Robert Dale Owen

The Wrong of Slavery, the Right of Emancipation, And the Future of the African Race in the United States

Robert Dale Owen

The Wrong of Slavery, the Right of Emancipation, And the Future of the African Race in the United States

ISBN/EAN: 9783744753678

Printed in Europe, USA, Canada, Australia, Japan

Cover: Foto ©ninafisch / pixelio.de

More available books at **www.hansebooks.com**

THE

WRONG OF SLAVERY

THE RIGHT OF EMANCIPATION

AND

THE FUTURE OF THE AFRICAN RACE
IN THE UNITED STATES.

BY

ROBERT DALE OWEN.

"Over the entire surface of the globe the races who compel others to labor, without laboring themselves, fall to decay."—COCHIN.

PHILADELPHIA:
J. B. LIPPINCOTT & CO.
1864.

PREFACE.

It is little more than three years since the first insurgent gun was fired against Fort Sumter: three years, as we reckon time; a generation, if we calculate by the stirring events and far-reaching upheavals that have been crowded into the eventful months.

Things move fast in days like these. War changes the legal relations of the combatants. War, in its progress, presents unlooked-for aspects of affairs, brings upon us necessities, opens up obligations. The rebellion—creator and teacher as well as scourge and destroyer—confers new rights, discharges from old bonds, imposes bounden duties.

Great questions come to the surface,—questions of national policy, demanding solution. In deciding some of these, we find little aid from precedent; for our condition as a nation is, to a certain extent, unprecedented.

We have been trying an experiment that never was tried in the world before. We have been trying to maintain a democratic government over thirty millions of people, of whom twenty millions existed under one system, industrial and social, ten millions under

2

another. The twenty millions, chiefly of one race, carried out among themselves a Declaration made eighty-eight years ago touching the equal creation and the inalienable rights of man. The ten millions consisted, in nearly equal portions, of two races,—one the descendants of voluntary emigrants who came hither seeking freedom and happiness in a foreign land; the other deriving their blood from ancestors against whom was perpetrated a terrible wrong, who came in chains and were sold as chattels. From these forced emigrants and their descendants were taken away almost all human rights, the right of life and of perpetuating a race of bondsmen excepted. Laws denied to them the rights of property, of marriage, of family, of education, of self-defence. The master-race sought to live by their labor.

The experiment we have been trying for more than three-quarters of a century was, whether, over social and industrial elements thus discordant, a republican government, asserting freedom in thought, in speech, in action, can be peacefully maintained.

Grave doubts, gloomy apprehensions, touching the nation's Future, have clouded the hopes of our wisest public men in days past. Even the statesmen of the Revolution saw on the horizon the cloud no bigger than a man's hand. Gradually it rose and spread and darkened. The tempest burst upon us at last.

Then some, faint-hearted and despairing of the Republic, prophesied that the good old days were gone, never to return. Others, stronger in hope and faith,

recognized, through the gloom, the correcting and re-
forming hand of God. They acknowledged that the
experiment had failed; but they confessed also that it
ought never to have succeeded. In adversity men
look into their hearts, there to read lessons which
prosperity had failed to teach them.

The experiment ought never to have succeeded, because it involved a grievous offence against Humanity
and Civilization. In peace, before the act of slaveholders made them public enemies, we scrupled to look
this offence in the face, seeing no remedy. But war,
which has its mission, opened our eyes and released
our hands. Times disturbed and revolutionary bring
their good as well as their evil. In such times abuses
ripen rapidly; their consequences mature, their ultimate results become apparent. We are reminded of
their transitory character. We are reminded that,
although for the time and in a certain stage of human
progress some abuses may have their temporary use,
and for this, under God's economy, may have been
suffered to continue, yet all abuses have but a limited
life: the Right only is eternal. Great, under such
circumstances, are our responsibilities; momentous
are the issues, for good or for evil, that hang upon our
decisions.

In this small volume, which busy men may read in
a few hours, I have sought to bring together, in condensed form, the facts and the law which bear upon
our present condition as a nation.

My task has led me over a vast field. In briefly tracing, from its inception in this hemisphere, the rise and progress of the great wrong which still threatens the life of the nation, I have followed the fortunes of a vast multitude, equal in number to the population, loyal and disloyal, black and white, of these United States. I have sketched, by the light of authentic documents, the dismal history of that multitude through three centuries and a half; seeking out their representatives, and inquiring into the numbers and the condition of these, at the present day. In so doing, I have arrived at conclusions which, to those who have never looked closely into the subject, may seem too marvellous for belief.

I invite a critical examination of my narrative and of the documents and statistics upon which rest its details and conclusions, not doubting that the candid reader will become convinced of its substantial truth. I have spared no pains to attain accuracy, well knowing that thus only can I expect to bring home the great lesson which such an episode in human history is eminently fitted to teach.

Passing, then, from the story of the wrong to look into its remedy, I have touched upon that inquiry in its various legal and constitutional aspects: as, the connection of slavery with the Constitution; how far that instrument admits, and how far it abstains from admitting, the existence of such a system; further, the character of what is termed slave-property; the right of emancipation in the insurrectionary States; the right of emancipation in the loyal slave States; the jurisdiction of the Supreme Court in the premises; the effect of the President's Emancipation Proclamation as well upon slaves within our lines as upon slaves still in the enemy's hands; and the force of that Proclamation both during war and after its conclusion.

In the same connection, I have treated of Emancipation as a great measure of national policy, essential to the preservation inviolate of the Constitution, indispensable to the re-establishment of peace, inseparable from the future maintenance, North and South, of domestic tranquillity.

In concluding this branch of the subject, I have spoken of Emancipation as a solemn national duty which, now that the constitutional obstacle has been removed, we cannot, consistently with what we owe to God and man, neglect or postpone. I have shown that our faith is pledged, and cannot be broken without bringing upon us the contempt of the civilized world.

Finally, after having traced the connection of the two races in the past, and set forth the duty of one race towards the other in the present, I have sought to look forward and inquire how they are likely, when both shall be free, to live together in the future; whether we shall have a race among us unwilling or unable to support itself; whether admixture of the races, both being free, is probable or desirable; whether, without admixture, the reciprocal social influence of the races on each other promises good or evil; what are the chances that a base prejudice of race shall diminish and disappear; and, lastly, whether, in case the colored man shall outlive that prejudice, disgraceful to us and depressing to him, and shall be clothed by law with the same rights in search of which we sought this Western World, there will be any thing in connection with his future in these United States to excite regret or inspire apprehension.

If to the lovers of the Union, to the friends of peace, to the adherents of lawful authority, I shall have supplied, in authentic form, facts and arguments such as may be employed to arouse the listless, to encourage the desponding, and to strengthen our country's cause, I shall ever be grateful for the opportunity that has been afforded me to bring these pages before the public.

It is proper I should here state that, in March, 1863, a commission—consisting of Colonel James McKaye, of New York, Dr. Samuel G. Howe, of Boston, and myself—was appointed by the Secretary of War, to examine and report upon the condition of the recently-emancipated freedmen of the United States; and that many of the materials for this volume are due to the joint investigations of that commission, and were embodied in the Final Report,* prepared by myself as chairman of the commission in question. I have to

---

* Two supplemental Reports, referred to in this work, were prepared and presented to the War Department,—one by Colonel McKaye, the other by Dr. Howe.

add my acknowledgments to the Secretary of War for the permission, kindly accorded to me, to use and publish these in such form as I might judge proper.

To my colleagues I am indebted for valuable emendations and corrections; to Mr. Benjamin P. Hunt, of Philadelphia, for the loan of part of his valuable library, rich in works on West Indian history and emancipation; and to the secretary of the commission, Mr. George T. Chapman, for important aid in the task of collecting and collating the historical and statistical data upon which are based some of the most important deductions set forth in the pages which follow.

TABLE OF CONTENTS.

CHAPTER IX.

CHAPTER X.

CHAPTER XI.

PART II.

EMANCIPATION.

CHAPTER I.

PAGE

Importance of the question in its connection with the peace
and the honor of the country—International law as binding as the Constitution—The International Code to be
humanely interpreted—A just war has for its object the
restoration of peace—But we may strike, through the subjects of a hostile Government, at the Government itself.

CHAPTER II.

How far is slavery recognized by the Constitution?—Laws
infringing rights must be unmistakably expressed, to induce a court of justice to infer such an intent—Fugitive-
slave law provision—Two classes of claims to service and
labor—Certain rights of property recognized, but of what
kind?—Is an apprentice or a slave an article of merchandise?—State action cannot determine the interpretation of
the Constitution—Claims to labor of slaves protected only
as far as are claims to labor of apprentices—Evident intention studiously to refrain from recognizing slavery, except as a claim to labor—A chief-justice's assertion irrele-
vant and without foundation—Claims to service and labor
in the nature of debts or *choses in action*—Popular phraseology misleads—Whither the doctrine leads that slavery in
all its phases is recognized by the Constitution—Clause regarding representation—Is an apprentice a slave during
apprenticeship?—Magnitude of interests involved cannot
alter Constitution—Constitution does not recognize ownership of one human being in another—Under what circumstances Emancipation is constitutional.

CHAPTER III.

Civil war defined—Inhabitants of nations engaged in civil

PART III.

THE FUTURE OF THE AFRICAN RACE IN THE UNITED
STATES.

· CHAPTER I.

revenge—Mutual influence for good of the races on each other, if justice prevail.

CHAPTER VII.

IMPORTANCE, NATIONALLY, THAT THE NEGRO BE TREATED WITH JUSTICE............ 222

To ill treat the negro is to give aid and comfort to the enemy—It withdraws laborers from Northern farms—Its effects resemble those of treason—Depth of baseness to ill treat defenders of the Union—Negro must fight for freedom if he is to obtain it—The worst scheme of false economy—The crucial test of civilization is our treatment of the lowly and feeble.

CHAPTER VIII.

THE FREEDMAN NEEDS MERE TEMPORARY AID AND SUPERVISION............ 226

Risk that under guise of guardianship a sort of slavery may reappear—Mere temporary aid needed by refugees—Halfway Emancipation a failure—No compulsory contracts nor statutory rates of wages—Let the freedman learn to stand alone.

CHAPTER IX.

THE SUM OF OUR DUTY TOWARDS THE NEGRO RACE............ 228

Give them a fair chance—Their best defence against tyranny in general laws, not in a special organization—Secure to them rights of person and property, relieve them of prejudice, save them from virtual re-enslavement, and let them take care of themselves—Thus their existence among us will be a national benefit.

APPENDIX............ 231
Note A.—Testimony in confirmation.
Note B.—Proposed form of Act of General Emancipation.

INDEX............ 239

PART I.

SLAVERY.

"THERE is one calamity which penetrated furtively into the world, and which was at first scarcely distinguishable amidst the ordinary abuses of power: it originated with an individual whose name history has not preserved: it was wafted, like some accursed germ, upon a portion of the soil; but it afterwards nurtured itself, grew without effort, and spread naturally with the society to which it belonged. This calamity is Slavery. Christianity suppressed slavery, but the Christians of the sixteenth century re-established it; as an exception, indeed, to their social system, and restricted to one of the races of mankind."—DE TOCQUEVILLE.

19

PART I.

SLAVERY.

CHAPTER I.

AS A LABOR SYSTEM.

THE greatest social and political problems of the world connect themselves, more or less intimately, with the subject of labor. A people who regard work as degradation, though arts and letters flourish among them, are but emerging from barbarism. It has been sometimes said, with much truth, that the grade of civilization in a nation may be measured by the position which it accords to woman: a stricter test is the degree of estimation in which labor is held there.

Our race, in its gradual advance from ignorance and evil to comparative knowledge and good, has not yet, even in countries the most favored, outlived an error fatal to true progress. Sometimes avowedly, more often practically, a certain stigma still attaches to human labor; to that labor from which, in one shape or other, the world receives every thing of good, of useful, of beautiful, that charms the senses or ministers to the wants of man; to which we owe life, and every thing that makes life desirable.

According to the structure of society in each country, this error is modified in form. In certain nations of continental Europe the great line of social demarcation is drawn between the titled classes, whether noble by birth or ennobled by royal creation, constituting the privileged; and all other persons, including merchants, though wealthy, and lawyers, though eminent, and authors, though popular, constituting the unprivileged. More liberal England begins to admit within the pale the distinguished and successful among the professional classes, and from the mercantile and literary ranks. We ourselves, professing to honor industry and talking occasionally of the nobility of labor, have opened somewhat wider, but only throughout a portion of our Republic, the door which admits within the precincts of respectability.

Only throughout a portion of our Republic. In fifteen of these United States the opinions, the feelings, the practice of the inhabitants, as regards laborers and labor itself, have been more perverted, have been less civilized, than in the most despotic countries of Europe.

In these States the class of working husbandmen has been degraded, both as regards civil rights and social position, below the Pariahs of India. This cannot happen in any nation without producing results fatal alike to its prosperity and to the moral worth and essential dignity of its population. The only doubt as to these results is, whether their influence has been more pernicious on the enslavers or on the enslaved.

CHAPTER II.

ENSLAVEMENT OF INDIANS.

The introduction into our hemisphere of this terrible element of social demoralization was almost coeval with its discovery by Europeans. It was in October of the year 1492 that Columbus first landed; and it was just eight years afterwards, in the month of October, 1500, that Francis de Bovadilla was guilty of two outrages:—one, the sending home, in chains, of the Great Discoverer; the other, the reducing to bondage of the gentle islanders whose fair land he discovered. Bovadilla "granted liberal donations of Indians to all who applied for them."*

The first year of the sixteenth century saw introduced into America that baneful system, abhorrent to Christian civilization, which was to spread and gather numbers and strength and influence, until, after more than three centuries and a half of evil growth, it was to bring a million of combatants into the field, to sacrifice on the field of battle hundreds of thousands of lives and thousands of millions of treasure.

There is scarcely a page in history so replete with horrors as that which records the inception of Slavery in this hemisphere. That terrible abuse caused, in an incredibly short period, the extinction of a race,—a race whom all the historians of that day concur in representing as the most kind and inoffensive and hospitable

---

* Robertson's History of America, London, 1792, vol. i. book 2, p. 222. Herrera, General History of the Vast Continent and Islands of America (Stevens's translation), London, 1725, vol. i. p. 244.

of mankind. Gold must be had; Columbus had been disgraced because he had failed to send home a sufficiency of it. His successors resolved to escape that imputation. The mines must be worked; and the forced labor of the feeble natives was employed to work them.

After a time, royal sanction was obtained for the act. Isabella,—just if severe,—who had issued orders that the Indians should be free from servitude and from molestation,* died in 1504; and in 1511 Ferdinand issued a decree of his Privy Council, declaring that, "after mature consideration of the Apostolic Bull and other titles by which the crown of Castile claimed the right to its possessions in the New World, the servitude of the Indians was warranted both by the laws of God and man."†

Thus was legalized that system of *repartimientos,* under which there had been previously assigned to each Spaniard, by an order on some cacique, a certain number of natives, who were to be instructed in the Catholic faith. What the character of their masters and teachers was may be gathered from the fact that Columbus himself, misled by his eagerness to people the continent he had discovered, had recommended the transportation to Hispaniola of malefactors convicted of the less atrocious capital crimes. "The prisons of Spain," says Robertson, "were drained to collect members for the intended colony."‡

---

* Ovando "was particularly charged by the queen that all the Indians of Hispaniola should be free from servitude, and that none should molest them."—HERRERA, vol. i. p. 247.

† Robertson's History of America, vol. i. p. 307. This decree was passed against the protest of the Dominicans, the abolitionists of those days.

‡ Robertson, vol. i. pp. 192, 193. Herrera, dec. i. lib. iii. c. 2.

We are not left to imagine the fate of the helpless wretches confided to such hands. Irving tells us :—

"They [the Indians] were separated the distance of several days' journey from their wives and children, and doomed to intolerable labor of all kinds, extorted by the cruel infliction of the lash. * * * 'When the Spaniards who superintended the mines were at their repasts,' says Las Casas, 'the famished Indians scrambled like dogs for any bone thrown to them.' * * * 'If they fled from this incessant toil and barbarous coercion, and took refuge in the mountains, they were hunted like wild beasts, scourged in the most inhuman manner, and laden with chains to prevent a second escape.'"*

Las Casas' terrible history is full of horrors, of which he himself was eye-witness. "I have found," says he, "many dead in the road, others gasping under the trees, and others, again, in the pangs of death, faintly crying, 'Hunger! hunger!'"†

"So intolerable," says Washington Irving, "were the toils and suffering inflicted upon this weak and un-offending race, that they sank under them, dissolving, as it were, from the face of the earth."‡

There is no exaggeration in this statement, incredible if it seem. Robertson confirms it, giving some general statistics on the subject. His words are :—

"The original inhabitants on whose labor the Spaniards in Hispaniola depended for their prosperity and even their existence, wasted so fast that the extinction of the whole race seemed to be inevitable. When Columbus discovered Hispaniola, the number of its in-

---

* Irving's Columbus, vol. ii. p. 427.
† Las Casas, Hist. Ind., lib. ii. cap. 14, MS. Quoted by Irving.
‡ Irving's Columbus, vol. ii. p. 428.

habitants was computed to be at least a million. They
were reduced to sixty thousand in fifteen years."*

This was in 1507. Scarcely half a generation had
elapsed since Europeans had found these people weak
and ignorant indeed, but simple, cheerful, and happy;
and, in that brief period, so atrocious had been the
cruelty of their treatment that *ninety-four out of every
hundred* of the victims sank and perished under it!

But the picture, in all its blackness, is not yet filled
up. The deaths had increased with such frightful
rapidity that the common operations of life were
arrested thereby. The dead laborers had to be replaced
by fresh victims. And then it was that, as the culmi-
nation of enormities that have left an indelible stain
on the Spanish name, an expedient was resorted to, into
the conception of which there entered not inhuman
barbarity alone, but treachery and blasphemy also.

This infamous expedient is ascribed to Ovando. At
all events, under his Governorship, in 1508, the King
(Ferdinand) "was advised," says Herrera, "that the
Lucayo Islands† being full of people, it would be con-
venient to carry them over to Hispaniola that they
might be instructed in the Christian religion and civilized." Ferdinand, perhaps deceived by this artifice,
more probably willing to connive at an act of violence
which policy represented as necessary, gave his assent
to the proposal. Herrera informs us in what manner
it was carried into effect:—

"The Spaniards who went in the first ships told those

---

* Robertson's America, vol. i. p. 262. It is from Herrera, the most
correct and intelligent of the Spanish historians of that period, that
Robertson's calculation is taken. There seems no reason to discredit it.
Other historians estimate the number of original inhabitants much higher.
Benzoni puts it at two millions.

† Now the Bahama Islands.

people that they came from Hispaniola, where the souls of their parents, kindred, and friends lived at their ease ; and if they would go see them, they should be carried over in these ships. For it is certain that the Indian nations believed that the soul is immortal, and that, when the body was dead, it went to certain places of delight, where it wanted for nothing that might give it satisfaction."*

"That simple people," says Robertson, "listened with wonder and credulity, and, fond of visiting their relatives and friends in that happy region, followed the Spaniards with eagerness. By this artifice over forty thousand were decoyed into Hispaniola to share in the sufferings which were the lot of the inhabitants of that island, and to mingle their groans and tears with that wretched race of men."†

By this expedient the number of Indians in Hispaniola was raised to one hundred thousand. But the work of human destruction went on. Nine years later, to wit, in 1517, Roderigo Albuquerque, being appointed principal officer to distribute the *repartimientos,* caused an enumeration of the Indians to be made. The number was found to be reduced to fourteen thousand. Six-sevenths had perished in nine years! The survivors were put up for sale in different lots. The secrets of their prison-house what tongue can ever reveal?

Such was the first advent in this hemisphere of that system under which human labor is stigmatized as a degradation. The mind cannot realize—the imagination shrinks from conceiving—the atrocious barbarities to which such a system must have given birth, ere a race of men could have perished in a single generation

---

* Herrera, vol. i. p. 325.
† Robertson, Hist. Amer., vol. i. p. 263.

before it; a terrible attestation to the immeasurable sufferings that may result from a single great crime.

Well has De Tocqueville said.—

"There is one calamity which penetrated furtively into the world, and which was at first scarcely distinguishable amidst the ordinary abuses of power: it originated with an individual whose name history has not preserved; it was wafted like some accursed germ upon a portion of the soil; but it afterwards nurtured itself, grew without effort, and spread naturally with the society to which it belonged. This calamity is Slavery. Christianity suppressed slavery, but the Christians of the sixteenth century re-established it,—as an exception, indeed, to their social system, and restricted to one of the races of mankind."*

That another race was not subjected to it—that the Indians of Hispaniola and of the adjacent islands escaped perpetual servitude—is due not to the forbearance of their oppressors, but to the tender mercies of Death, the great liberator.

CHAPTER III.

SUBSTITUTION OF THE AFRICAN FOR THE INDIAN.

An incident to which is popularly ascribed the first substitution of the African negro for the native of Hispaniola—the first introduction, therefore, among us of that race who were to be thenceforth for centuries branded with the mark of Cain—may teach us how humanity, in her aberrations, sometimes with the best in-

---

* Democracy in America, by De Tocqueville (Cambridge edition, 1862), vol. i. p. 457.

tentions, aids in laying broad the foundations of misery
and of crime.

Bartolomeo de las Casas, a Dominican monk, had
accompanied Columbus on his second voyage. A man
of eminent benevolence and quick sensibilities, the sufferings of the downtrodden Indians produced upon him
a profound impression. After spending many years in
Hispaniola, in fruitless efforts to ameliorate the condition of the natives, he returned to Spain previous to
the death of Ferdinand, was favorably received by that
monarch and by his minister the Cardinal Ximenes,
and succeeded in procuring the appointment of three
Superintendents of the Colonies, to whom he himself
was joined, with the well-earned title of "Protector of
the Indians." The mission, however, was of small avail.
The Spaniards of Hispaniola opposed every obstacle, representing that without compulsion the Indians would
not labor, and that without their labor the colony could
not subsist. Finding no countenance in the island, Las
Casas again returned to Spain, where he arrived shortly
before the death of Ximenes, and found Charles V. suc-
cessor of Ferdinand.

Then it was, after a vain endeavor to procure the
freedom of the aborigines, that Las Casas, thinking
that a hardier race than they would suffer less as slaves,[*]
recommended to Ximenes the policy of supplying the
labor-market of Hispaniola with negroes from the
Portuguese settlements on the African coast.

This, though affirmed by Robertson,[†] following Her-

---

[*] Herrera (dec. i. lib. 9, c. 5) affirms that one negro was considered
equal, as laborer, to four Indians.

[†] Robertson's History of America, vol. i. p. 321. The censure conveyed
in the words of this author, when he says of Las Casas, "In the warmth
of his zeal to save the aborigines from the yoke, he pronounced it to
be lawful and expedient to impose one still heavier on the Africans,"

rera, is denied by several modern authors of repute.* But the simple fact that Las Casas did make such a proposal, though not until after a certain number of African slaves had been imported into the New World, is beyond denial,—seeing that it has been stated, and nobly atoned for, so far as frank acknowledgment of error can atone, by Las Casas himself, writing his own history shortly before his death, in that retirement to which, after years of fruitless exertion in behalf of the suffering natives, he betook himself. These, literally translated, are his words:—

"This advice, that license be given to bring negro slaves to these lands, the ecclesiastic Casas first gave, not taking note of the injustice with which the Portuguese seize them and make them slaves; which advice, after he had reflected on the matter, he would not have given for all he possessed in the world. For he always held that they were made slaves unjustly and tyrannically, seeing that the same rule applies in their case as in that of the Indians."†

---

implies, when given thus without explanation, too harsh a judgment of a good man.

* Doelinger (Hist. Eccl., vol. iii. sect. 160, p. 397) makes an argument, with evidence adduced, in proof that the imputation is unjust. Cochin discredits the charge, stating that in the debates which Las Casas was forced to sustain against Quevedo, Bishop of Darien, and also against the confessor and historian of Charles, Sepulveda, "this opinion is found neither on his lips nor on those of his adversaries."—L'Abolition de l'Esclavage, vol. i. p. 286. The explanation of this may be, that by that time he had repented the advice which a few years before he had given.

† "Esto aviso de que se diese licencia para traer esclavos negros á estas tierras, dió primero el clérigo Casas, no advirtiendo la injusticia con que los Portugueses los toman y hacen esclavos; el qual despues de que cayó en ello no lo diera por quanto habia en el mundo. Porque siempre los tuvo por injusta y tiránicamente hechos esclavos: porque la misma razon es de ellos que de los Indios."—LAS CASAS: Hist. de las Indias, lib. 3, tom. 2, cap. 101. Las Casas here speaks of himself in the third person.

Ximenes, whether from motives of policy or humanity, rejected Las Casas' proposal, dying soon after.

Las Casas renewed the proposal, after Ximenes' death, to the ministers of Charles, by whom it was more favorably received. And, the officers of the "India House of Seville" having recommended four thousand as the proper number to be sent,* the young king acted upon the recommendation. In accordance with the monopoly-favoring policy of that age, Charles granted to one of his Flemish favorites a patent for the importation into the colonies of four thousand negro slaves. That patent was sold to a company of Genoese merchants, who, about the year 1517, carried it into effect.

This, as regards America, was the germ of a traffic, the foulest blot on the history of Christendom ; a traffic carried on, in defiance of law, human and divine, to exempt from labor one race of men at expense of brutal degradation to another; a traffic that has brought upon the American hemisphere a moral curse worse than war, pestilence, or famine, and which, as to every nation that persists in it, leads,—ever must lead,—sooner or later, by one way or another, to national ruin.

---

* "The suggestion of Las Casas was approved by the Chancellor and by Adrian, the colleague of the late Cardinal (Ximenes), and indeed it is probable that there was hardly a man of that time who would have seen further than the excellent clerigo did. Las Casas was asked what number of negroes would suffice. He replied that he did not know; upon which a letter was sent to the officers of the India House of Seville, to ascertain the fit number, in their opinion. They said that four thousand would at present suffice,—being one thousand for each of the islands, Hispaniola, San Juan, Cuba, and Jamaica."—*Conquerors of the New World and their Bondsmen*, London, 1852.

CHAPTER IV.

NUMBER OF SLAVES SHIPPED FROM AFRICA.

THE statistical details are lacking which might enable us to form a strictly accurate numerical estimate of the victims to this detestable trade, the operations of which extended through three centuries and a half,—diminishing, however, during the last quarter of a century, and soon, we may confidently hope, to cease forever. An approximating estimate of the number of negroes transported to America is all that can now be obtained.

The *asientos*, treaties, or contracts of the Spanish government for the supply of its American colonies with slaves, commencing in 1517, were occasionally granted throughout the sixteenth century, and multiplied in the seventeenth and eighteenth. Some were to individuals, some to companies, some to governments.

Nothing more strongly marks the character of these treaties for the delivery of human beings than the terms employed in wording them. An asiento was granted, in 1696, to the Portuguese Guinea Company, by which that company bound itself to deliver to Spain, in her transatlantic colonies, *ten thousand tons of negroes.** England, to designate the human chattels she agreed to supply, employed a term such as vendors of broadcloth or calico might use. By treaty with Spain, bearing date March 26, 1713, his Britannic Majesty undertook to introduce into Spanish America one hundred and fourteen thousand *pieces of India*, of both sexes and all

---

* " *Diez mil toneladas de negros*" is the expression in the original. The text can be found in the Cantillo collection, p. 32.

ages.* These various treaties, concluded in the name of the Most Holy Trinity,† contained not one article, not a single provision of any kind, for the humane treatment or for the protection from outrage of the human merchandise therein stipulated to be delivered.‡

The extent of these treaties, and their lucrative character to the Spanish crown, may be gathered from the following :—

"A single government, Spain, which assumes the name of Catholic, concluded in less than two centuries more than ten treaties to authorize, protect, and profit by the transportation of more than half a million of human beings. It levied on each of these human heads, reckoning them by the piece or by the ton, a tax which amounted in the aggregate to upwards of fifty millions of francs"§ (say ten millions of dollars).

The above treaties were with England, France, and Portugal,—the grants to individuals and to companies not being included.

In the middle of the eighteenth century the English slave-trade, which up to that time had been more or less of a monopoly, was thrown open. Statute 23 George II. (that is, in 1750) c. 31, after reciting that the "African slave-trade is very advantageous to Great Britain," enacts that "it shall be lawful for all His Majesty's subjects to trade and traffic to and from any

---

* "*Piezas de Indias*" are the words in the Spanish text.—*Abolition de l'Esclavage*, par Cochin, tom. ii. p. 286. This treaty gave England a monopoly of the slave-trade to Spanish colonies for thirty years,—namely, from 1713 to 1744.

† "El nombre del santisima Trinidad."

‡ After enumerating the various *asientos* made by Spain, Cochin says, "Dans tous ces traités, pas une disposition, pas une syllabe destinée à defendre ces malheureux contre les abus et les souffrances."— *Work cited*, vol. ii. p 288.

§ Work cited, vol. ii. p. 288.

port or place in Africa between the port of Sallee, in South Barbary, and the Cape of Good Hope."

Great Britain, the first to abolish this infamous traffic, was, previous to its abolition, the most extensively engaged in it. Her connection with it, the manner and extent to which it was conducted, together with many statistical details, imperfect indeed, but instructive as far as they go, are set forth in a ponderous folio volume published by official authority in the year 1789,—being a *"Report of the Lords of the Committee of Council,* appointed for the consideration of all matters relating to trade and foreign plantations, submitting to His Majesty's consideration the evidence and information they have collected in consequence of His Majesty's Order in Council, dated February 11, 1788, concerning the present state of the trade to Africa, and particularly the trade in slaves; and concerning the effects and consequences of this trade, as well in Africa and the West Indies, as to the general commerce of this kingdom."

There can be no safer document than this from which to draw information such as it contains. The Lords composing this Committee of Council gave the slave-holders ample opportunity to state their case, both by testimony and argument. Three-fourths, at least, of the witnesses examined are slave-dealers or captains of slavers. They admit also, it is true, testimony and documentary evidence (especially as to deaths of sailors on slave-ships) offered by the celebrated Thomas Clarkson; but they scrupulously abstain from all opinions in regard to the slave-trade and from all recommendations or suggestions touching its abolition.

In this volume we find two estimates as to the number of negroes then (namely, in 1788) annually carried to the American colonies: the first puts it at eighty thousand annually; the second, containing a detailed estimate of slaves annually sold at sixteen different points on the African coast, sums up seventy-four thousand.* Of these one-half are said to be procured on the Gold Coast, at Bonny and New Calabar and at Loango, Melimba and Cabenda,—about thirty-eight thousand set down as purchased by the British, twenty thousand by the French, ten thousand by the Portuguese, and the rest by the Danes and Dutch.

It would appear, from a statistical table given in another part of the same volume, that these estimates fall short of the truth. This table gives the total number of vessels sailing annually from Liverpool from the year 1751 to the year 1787, distinguishing the slavers and giving their tonnage; from which it appears that about *one-tenth* of all the vessels that sailed from that port during the above thirty-six years were engaged in the slave-trade, and that their tonnage ran up from a little over five thousand tons in 1751 to about fifteen thousand in 1786 and 1787.† But, as we shall show hereafter, the number of slaves carried averaged over two to a ton: consequently, British ships from the port of Liverpool alone carried upwards of thirty thousand annually.

Another table‡ shows that the tonnage of African slavers from all the ports of Great Britain was, in 1787, twenty-two thousand two hundred and sixty-three tons.

---

* The first is contained in the testimony of Mr. Penny (Report, Part I. Sheet I); the second, in that of Mr. Norris (Report, Part I. Sheet K). The table in detail is given Part IV. No. 14. The volume not being paged (except as to a single brief document contained in it, to wit, Minutes of Evidence before a Committee of the Whole House), more exact references cannot be given.

† Lords of Council Report; Minutes of Evidence before Committee of the Whole House, p. 49.

‡ Lords of Council Report, Part IV. No. 1.

Consequently, the annual number of slaves transported to America, at that time, in British bottoms, was upwards of forty-five thousand, instead of thirty-eight thousand as estimated. In this proportion the total estimate, including vessels of all countries, would be run up to nearly ninety thousand slaves a year. It would appear, from other evidence, that even this is below the actual number.

The calculations produced before the French Committee of Inquiry of 1848 place the number of slaves exported from 1788 to 1840 at from one hundred thousand to one hundred and forty thousand a year, and from 1840 to 1848 at from fifty thousand to eighty thousand.*

The rate after 1848 continued to diminish. Nevertheless, in 1860 it was still nearly thirty thousand a year.†

These figures enable us to calculate, with approximate accuracy, the extent of the slave-trade from 1788 to 1860; that is to say, for the seventy-two last years of its course, thus:—

Annual deportation of slaves from the year 1788 to the year 1840,
say fifty-two years, at an average of one hundred and twenty
thousand a year.. 6,240,000

---

* See Cochin, vol. ii. p. 310.

Lord Palmerston, from his place in the House of Lords, July 26, 1844, said, "According to the Report of Messrs. Vendervelt and Buxton, from one hundred and twenty thousand to one hundred and fifty thousand slaves are landed annually in America."

This calculation applied to the early years of the present century.

† "When we remember that one hundred and forty thousand were yearly carried away from Africa, while this year the number has not reached thirty thousand, we should neither deny the progress nor abandon the hope of a complete suppression of this traffic."—*Speech of Lord John Russell, in Parliament.* June 8, 1860.

"At least thirty thousand slaves are annually imported into Cuba."—*Speech of Mr. Cave, in Parliament,* June 8, 1860.

Annual deportation from 1840 to 1848, say eight years, at an
average of sixty-five thousand a year............................   520,000
Annual deportation from 1848 to 1860, say twelve years, at an
average of thirty thousand a year............................   360,000

Total in seventy-two years...................... 7,120,000

What annual rate we ought to assume as a fair average for the two centuries preceding 1788, during which, as Cochin reminds us, "all Europe abandoned itself openly to the negro slave-trade,"* it is somewhat difficult to determine. In the Report by the Lords of the Committee of Council, already referred to, is a table† showing the annual importation of slaves throughout seventy-four years of that period (namely, from 1702 to 1775 both inclusive) into a single English colony, to wit, the island of Jamaica. The total is four hundred and ninety-seven thousand seven hundred and thirty-six, being an average of six thousand seven hundred and twenty-six a year. Nor is there a regular increase; for in the decade from 1720 to 1730 there were as many imported as in the last ten years of the term,—the average for each of the years in either decade being about seven thousand seven hundred.

But I shall hereafter furnish proof that to the number of slaves delivered in the colonies we must add at least twenty-five per cent. to obtain the number shipped on the African coast. This would bring up the annual average exported from Africa for Jamaica to eight thousand four hundred and seven.

If we assume the total deportation of slaves from Africa in the year 1788 to have been one hundred thousand, which is the French Committee's lowest estimate

---

* "Au dix-septième et au dix-huitième siècle l'Europe entière se livre ouvertement à la traite des noirs."—COCHIN, L'Abolition de l'Esclavage, tom. ii. p. 281.

† Lords of Council Report, Jamaica, Appendix, Part III. Sheet. P.

for any year from 1788 to 1840, and if we suppose that there were annually exported, during each year of the two centuries preceding 1788, two-fifths only of that number, say forty thousand, we shall be assuming the annual total throughout these two centuries at less than five times the number that we know to have been annually exported during seventy-four years of that period to supply the single island of Jamaica. So far as, at this distance of time, and with the scanty materials before us, one can judge, the estimate is a moderate one.*

Previous to the year 1588, that is to say, for eighty years after the beginning of the negro slave-trade probably about 1508, the true average is still more uncertain. The Spanish *asientos* of the sixteenth century were usually for the delivery of from three thousand to five thousand negroes annually. Let us assume the entire slave-trade by all nations during that period at five thousand negroes only, for each year.

Adopting the data above suggested, we obtain the following general results :—

Total Deportation of Negroes by the Slave-Trade, from the year 1508 *to the year* 1860.

From 1508 to 1588, eighty years, at an average of five thousand a year..	400,000
From 1588 to 1788, two hundred years, at an average of forty thousand a year..	8,000,000
From 1788 to 1860, seventy-two years, as already estimated....	7,120,000
Total in three hundred and fifty-two years..............	15,520,000

* By a table, already referred to (Part IV. No. 1) in the Report of the Lords of Council, it appears that as early as 1701, *one hundred and four* British vessels were employed in the slave-trade. The number, however, varied very widely in different years, the lowest number (in 1715) being but twenty-four, and the highest (in 1771) being one hundred and ninety-two. The table was obtained from the Inspector-General of Imports and Exports.

Upwards of fifteen millions and a half of human beings forcibly torn from their native country, and doomed to perpetual slavery—themselves and their offspring—in a foreign land !*

---

* I have endeavored, in the above estimate, to avoid error, except it be on the side of moderation. Very reputable authorities put the importations in the seventeenth and eighteenth centuries considerably higher than I have assumed them. Bancroft, who appears to have carefully investigated the matter, says:—

"The English slave-trade began to attain its great activity after the *Asiento* treaty. [That treaty was dated March 26, 1713.] From 1680 to 1700, the English took from Africa about three hundred thousand negroes, or about fifteen thousand a year. The number, during the continuance of the *Asiento*, may be averaged not far from thirty thousand. [It continued for thirty years, to wit, from 1713 to 1744.] Raynal considers the number of negroes exported by all European nations from Africa before 1776, to have been nine millions; and the considerate German historian of the slave-trade, Albert Hüne, deems his statement too small. A careful analysis of the colored population of America at different periods and the inference to be deduced from the few authentic records of the numbers imported, corrected by a comparison with the authentic products of slave-labor, as appearing in the annals of English commerce, seem to prove, beyond a doubt, that even the estimate of Raynal is larger than the reality."—*Bancroft's History of the United States*, vol. iii. p. 412.

Raynal's estimate, thought too low by Hüne, is nine millions up to 1776; and, as the exportations averaged about eighty thousand a year from 1776 to 1788, that would give a million more, bringing his calculation up to *ten millions* if extended to 1788. But my estimate, as above, up to that year, is but eight millions four hundred thousand,—that is, upwards of a million and a half, or just sixteen per cent., below Raynal's.

Bancroft thinks that we shall not err much if in the century previous to 1776 we assume the number imported by the English to have been three millions. But I have assumed the total imported by all nations in the two centuries preceding 1788 to have been eight millions. Bancroft estimates importation *in a single century by one nation only at three millions.* I estimate importation *in two centuries by all nations at eight millions.* The probability will be conceded that the former estimate is at a higher rate, in proportion, than the latter.

CHAPTER V.

HOW SLAVES WERE OBTAINED IN AFRICA.

But we cannot attain to a just conception of the aggregate of evil and suffering produced by this gigantic outrage upon human rights, nor of the loss of life attendant thereon, without considering, first, the mode in which slaves were supplied to the European traders, secondly, the manner in which they were transported to their destination, and, thirdly, the result, especially in its influence on population, in the slave colonies.

As to the two first subjects, the Report of the Lords of Council—unimpeachable testimony—furnishes many suggestive particulars.

It is proved, in the first place, that the sources whence slaves were obtained on the African coast were,—

First. As prisoners of war.

The evidence as to this source of supply was obtained from almost all the witnesses who had visited the African coast.

Major-General Rooke said, "When a ship arrived to purchase slaves, the King of Demel sent to the chiefs of the villages in his dominions to send him a given number; but if they were not to be procured on this requisition, the king went to war till he got as many as he wanted." During his stay at Goree of four or five months, he heard of two battles being fought for slaves.*

Captain T. Wilson, employed on the business of Government in 1783 and 1784, states, as to the kingdom

---

* Lords of Council Report, Part I. Sheet G.

of Demel, "When they were at war, they made pri-soners and sold them; and when they were not at war, they made no scruple of taking any of their own sub-jects and selling them, even whole villages at once. * * * He has been told that the King of Demel can bring seventy thousand or eighty thousand men into the field."*

Captain Hills :—"There was scarcely an evening in which he did not see people go out in war-dresses to obtain slaves from the neighboring villages." This was at Goree.†

"The manner in which Sir George Yonge understood that slaves became so is first as prisoners of war; and these he thinks are the greatest number." This was in Senegal and Gambia; "but the same account was given to him all along the coast."‡

The Rev. Mr. Newton :—"The greater number of slaves are captives made in war."§

Mr. Dalrymple says, "One of the modes of making slaves, adopted by the kings and great men, is by breaking up a village,—that is, setting fire to it and seizing the people as they escape. This occurs some-times in a neighbor's territory, more frequently in their own. The practice is notorious." The witness speaks of Gambia and countries adjoining.‖

Another mode of procuring slaves is akin to this. They are *panyared*, to employ the phrase of the coun-try,—that is, kidnapped by individuals.

Dr. A. Sparrman, Inspector of the Royal Museum at Stockholm, and a traveller in the interior of Africa,

---

* Lords of Council Report, Part I. Sheet G.
† Report cited, Part I. Sheet G.
‡ Report cited, Part I. Sheet H.
§ Report cited, Part I. Sheet I.
‖ Report cited, Part I. Sheet G.

deposed, "They seize one another in the night when they have an opportunity, and sometimes invite each other to their houses and there detain and sell them to the European traders. * * * The number of persons so kidnapped is considerable. He himself witnessed two instances."*

Mr. Falconbridge, surgeon of slaver, testifies, "On the windward coast the negroes are afraid of stirring out at night, lest they be kidnapped. A woman, big with child, told him she was caught as she was returning from a neighbor's house."†

Mr. Devoynes says, speaking of the Gold Coast, "The greater part of the slaves are brought from the interior: they are sold from hand to hand, and many of them come a great distance,—it is said, from eight hundred to nine hundred miles."‡

The next source of supply is the selling of criminals. The universal testimony is that the chief crimes for which they are sold are adultery, theft, and witch-craft,—sometimes for murder. Occasionally they are sold for debt. Some stake their liberty in gambling, and are sold if they lose.

Admiral Edwards said, "Adultery is the crime for which they are most usually sold. In this case the person offended has a claim not only to the man and woman offending, and to all their property, but also to their family and slaves."§

Theft is common among them. One witness (Mr. Dalzell) testifies that he purchased a son of his father, who sold him to avoid the punishment which the son

---

* Lords of Council Report, Part I. Sheet G.
† Report cited, Part I. Sheet N.
‡ Report cited, Part I. Sheet K.
§ Report cited, Part I. Sheet L.

had incurred for stealing from a white man; which, the witness adds, "is never pardoned." This was in the kingdom of Dahomey.*

A witness (Mr. Weaver) explained that "they understand by witchcraft the power of doing mischief by supernatural means."† Another witness (Mr. Mathews) testifies that, having refused to purchase a man suspected of witchcraft, who was offered to him for sale, "they tied a stone around his neck and threw him into the sea."‡

The Rev. Mr. Baggs, chaplain to Commodore Thompson during two voyages (in 1783 and 1784), says, of the African coast generally, "The revenue of the kings of the country depends on the sale of slaves. They therefore strain every nerve to accuse and condemn. Their codes of law are made subservient to the slave-trade."§

Mr. Penny deposes, "Some are made slaves in consequence of gaming, of which they are very fond. They stake themselves; first a leg, then an arm, lastly the head; and when they have lost that, they surrender themselves as slaves. If a man stake and lose a leg only, he continues gambling until he has lost the whole of himself, or is cleared."||

There is no evidence that slaves were bred for sale. The concurrent testimony is against it.

There is abundant testimony in proof that as to negroes offered for sale as slaves and rejected by the slave-dealers on account of their state of health or

---

* Lords of Council Report, Part I. Sheet L.

† Report cited, Part I. Sheet L.

‡ Report cited, Part I. Sheet I.

§ Report cited, Part I. Sheet N, 5.

|| Report cited, Part I. Sheet I.

otherwise, their fate is usually a sad one. Even delay
in the market may cause their death.

The Rev. Mr. Baggs said, "He had proof that when
marauding parties come with their booty in slaves to
the coast, and find no vessel, they kill the slaves
because of the expense of sending them back."*

Mr. Falconbridge said, "He has seen slaves who
were offered for sale and refused cruelly beaten."†

Mr. Penny, who had made eleven voyages as captain
of slavers, deposes, "He has been repeatedly informed
that slaves bought for sale and rejected by the slave-
dealers on account of disease or otherwise are destroyed
as not worth their food."‡

Sir George Yonge " saw a beautiful child, about five
years old, brought from the Bullam shore, opposite
Sierra Leone. As the child was too young to be an
object of trade, the persons who had him to sell gave
him no food, and threatened to throw him into the river.
Sir George, to save his life, offered a quarter-cask of
Madeira for him, which was accepted,—brought him to
England, and made a present of him to the Marquis of
Landsdown. He understood this child had been kid-
napped."§

Mr. Arnold, surgeon on board a slaver, testified,
"One day a woman, with a child in her arms, was
brought to us to be sold. The captain refused to purchase her, not wishing to be plagued with a child on
board: so she was taken back to shore. On the following morning she was again brought to us, but
without the child, and apparently in great sorrow.

---

* Lords of Council Report, Part I. Sheet N, 5.
† Report cited, Part I. Sheet M.
‡ Report cited, Part I. Sheet I.
§ Report cited, Part I. Sheet II.

The black trader admitted that the child had been killed in the night to accommodate the sale."*

What a lifting of the veil upon a terrible series of atrocities is there, even in these brief extracts, coldly and dispassionately worded as they are! For what a catalogue of crimes were they responsible who sent slavers to the African coast! What wars have they not stirred up! What murders instigated! What temptations have they not presented to the cupidity of savage sovereign and subject alike! If the King of Dahomey, or some other royal barbarian, perverted criminal law to obtain convictions as a source of revenue,—if a black trader put to death the infant that the mother might be salable,—who were the tempters to such acts? who the original authors of this wickedness? The horrors of the Middle Passage were surpassed by those that necessarily preceded it.

The ministers of the British Crown cannot be accused of sentimentalism. They are no declaimers, no propagandists, no extremists in speculative philanthropy. Their humanity is tempered with moderation and suggested by official evidence. Yet with what perseverance have they labored, even to the present day, after themselves abolishing the slave-trade in 1807, to procure its subsequent abolition by all civilized nations! Within twenty-five years—to wit, between 1818 and 1842—they concluded twenty-three treaties on the subject, with Holland, Sweden, Denmark, Russia, Austria, Prussia, Naples, Tuscany, Sardinia, the Hanse Towns, the United States, Hayti, Texas, Mexico, Colombia, New Granada, Venezuela, Ecuador, Uruguay, Buenos Ayres, Chili, Peru, and Bolivia.

---

* Lords of Council Report, Part I. Sheet N, 4.

Lord Palmerston, speaking in the House of Lords in 1844, gave some of the reasons which stirred the Government to move in this matter. He said :—

"The negroes destined for the slave-trade are not taken from the neighborhood where they are embarked. A great number come from the interior. Many are captives made in wars excited by thirst for the gain procured by the sale of the prisoners. But the greatest number arise from kidnapping expeditions, and an organized system of man-stealing in the interior of Africa.

"When the time approaches to set out with the slave-caravans for the coast, the kidnappers surround a peaceful village at night, set it on fire, and seize on the inhabitants, killing all who resist. If the village attacked is situated on a mountain offering facilities for flight, and the inhabitants take refuge in the caverns, the kidnappers kindle large fires at the entrance; and those who are sheltered there, placed between death by suffocation and slavery, are forced to give themselves up. If the fugitives take refuge on the heights, the assailants render themselves masters of all the springs and wells, and the unfortunates, devoured by thirst, return to barter liberty for life.

"The prisoners made, they proceed to the choice. The robust individuals of both sexes, and the children of above six or seven years of age, are set aside to form part of the caravan which is to be driven to the sea-shore. They rid themselves of the children under six years by killing them on the spot, and abandon the aged and infirm, thus condemning them to die of hunger.

"The caravan sets out. Men, women, and children traverse the burning sands and rocky defiles of the mountains of Africa barefoot and almost naked. The feeble are stimulated by the whip; the strong are secured by chaining them together or placing them under a yoke. Many fall from exhaustion on the road, and die, or become the prey of wild beasts.

"On reaching the sea-shore, they are penned up, and crowded together in buildings called *barracoons*, where they fall a prey to epidemics. Death often cruelly thins their ranks before the arrival of a slave-trader."*

Lord Palmerston's general deduction from these and other facts connected with the trade is contained in the same speech. "It is calculated," he says, "that of three negroes seized in the interior of Africa, to be sent into slavery, but one reaches his destination: the two others die in the course of the operations of the slave-trade. Whatever may be the number yearly landed, therefore, we must triple it to obtain the true number of human beings which this detestable traffic annually carries off from Africa."

A portion of the facts which form the data of such a calculation remain to be considered,—the manner, namely, of stowing and of treating negroes in slave-ships, and the mortality thence resulting.

---

* Speech of Lord Palmerston, delivered in the House of Lords, July 26, 1844.

CHAPTER VI.

HOW SLAVES WERE TRANSPORTED FROM AFRICA.

THE Report of the Lords in Council, from which I have already so copiously quoted, furnishes exact and conclusive evidence as to the space commonly allowed to slaves during their passage.

The vessels employed were usually from one hundred to two hundred and fifty or three hundred tons burden,—averaging, in early times, little over one hundred tons, but towards the end of the eighteenth century being of the capacity of one hundred and fifty or two hundred tons. The universal testimony is that the average number carried per ton was *two persons and upwards.*

John Anderson, master of slaver, "conceives that two slaves to a ton cannot crowd a ship."

Sir George Yonge (of the British Navy) says, "The usual allowance of space is two slaves to a ton, *sometimes three.* If two were allowed to a ton, he thought there would be room enough."

A bill had been introduced into Parliament, which proposed to limit the number for each ton. Evidence was taken as to its effect, resulting as follows.

James Penny had made eleven voyages as captain of slaver He was asked, "If the blank of the bill is filled with one and a half to a ton, will it, in your opinion, tend to the abolition of the trade?" Answer, "I am clearly of opinion that it will."*

This witness handed in a table, of which the accuracy was afterwards endorsed by Mr. Tarleton, a Liverpool

---

* Lords of Council Report, Minutes of Evidence, p. 41.

merchant extensively engaged in the slave-trade, exhibiting the estimate of profit or loss on a vessel of one hundred tons, at different rates of slaves per ton. Here it is:—

	STERLING.		
	£.	s.	d.
At one man per ton, the loss is	590	1	
At one man and a half per ton, the loss is	206	19	9
At two men per ton, the profit is	180	3	6
At two men and a half per ton, the profit is	761	5	6*

James Jones, six years captain of a slaver, deposed, "If a ship of two hundred tons does not purchase four hundred slaves and more, she must certainly sink the owners' money." He was asked, "What measurement do the merchants allow for each slave?" Answer, "In a ship of two hundred tons and under, merchants all carry more than two slaves to each ton." Being asked what width was allowed, at that rate, to each slave, when stowed below, he answered, "A full-grown slave takes sixteen inches in width; smaller slaves, twelve to fourteen inches."†

John Matthews, seventeen years in the slave-trade, was asked, "What space in length and breadth do you consider sufficient for the health and comfort of the negroes on board?" Answer, "The space they occupy when they lie on their backs is always considered sufficient for them." When asked for the number of inches, he at first refused to give it, saying he did not know. Afterwards he gave fourteen and two-third inches as a fair average.‡

Another slave-captain (James Bowen) expressed a different opinion. He said, "The average number of

---

* Lords of Council Report, Minutes of Evidence, p. 21.
† Report cited, Minutes of Evidence, pp. 44, 45.
‡ Report cited, Minutes of Evidence, pp. 24, 25.

slaves carried is two to a ton. * * * Is of opinion that the greatest number of slaves which a ship can carry consistent with their preservation *is not above one per ton.*"*

James Penny, a part of whose evidence has already been quoted, said, " The average allowance of width to a slave is fourteen inches and two-thirds."

Captain Parrey was sent to Liverpool by Government, in 1788, to take the dimensions of ships employed in the African trade. A plan and sections are given of one of these, the Brooks, a ship of two hundred and ninety-seven tons burden, well known in the trade. The room said by her owners to be allowed for each slave was —

For men, each, six feet by sixteen inches.

For women, each, five feet ten inches by sixteen inches.

For boys, each, five feet by fourteen inches.

For girls, each, four feet six inches by twelve inches.

At these rates Captain Parrey found that she could carry four hundred and seventy slaves. But she *did* carry six hundred and seven, being about two to a ton. This reduces the width actually allowed to the men to less than *twelve inches and a half,* and the rest in proportion.†

What terrible glimpses of human suffering are furnished by these dry, mathematical details! The slaver,

---

* Lords of Council Report, Part III. Sheet d.

† Mr. William James, who had made three voyages on slavers, testified "that on board the Britannia the height between decks was about five feet and a half. No slave whatever had room to turn himself when the cargo was completed. The chief mate, boatswain, and an active young man were employed in stowing or packing them together,—as in adjusting their arms and legs and prescribing a fixed space for each."—*Lords' Report,* Part II. Sheet d, 7.

to make money, *must* stow his human cargo with twelve to sixteen inches only of board for each to lie on! Lord Palmerston, speaking of African slave-ships, strikingly says, "A negro has not as much room in them as a corpse in a coffin."*

As the witnesses examined by the Lords in Council were, for the most part, masters or surgeons of slavers or merchants engaged in the trade, the results of this frightful system only occasionally come to light. The slaves, thus stowed away like so much inanimate cargo, often felt their lives so grievous a burden that they attempted suicide, sometimes by throwing themselves overboard, sometimes by refusing all food. To prevent the first mode of self-destruction, as well as to avoid the dangers of insurrection, the men-slaves were always put in irons, fastened two and two, the "chains being locked, at different intervals, to the deck,"† and when released and brought on deck, as they were every fine day, were compelled, by fear of the lash, to exercise— to *dance*, as the phrase of the trade was—in their fetters.‡ As to the second mode of suicide, by self-inflicted starvation, its frequency rendered it an object of suspicion and of punishment. Captain Hall, a slave-trader, deposes, "Has known instances of slaves being punished for not eating, supposed to be from stubbornness, when in reality it was from indisposition ; and in some instances the slaves so punished have been found dead next morning."§

---

* Speech, already quoted, of July 26, 1844.

† Testimony of John Newton, mate of slaver.—*Lords' Report*, Part II. Sheet b, 2.

‡ "While the slaves are upon deck, it is thought necessary that they should take exercise, for which purpose the chief mate and boatswain are stationed with a cat-of-nine-tails, to compel them to dance, as it is called."—*Testimony of William Jones*, Lords' Report, Part II. Sheet d, 7.

§ Lords' Report, Part II. Sheet c, 2.

The women and children were not chained, and had usually more liberty than the men. But a surgeon of a slaver (Mr. James Arnold) thus indicates the spirit in which they were sometimes treated. "When the women were sitting by themselves below, he had heard them singing, but always, at these times, in tears. Their songs contained the history of their separation from friends and country. These songs were so disagreeable to the captain that he has taken them up and flogged them in so terrible a manner for no other reason than this, that he (Mr. Arnold) has been a fortnight or three weeks in healing the incisions made."*

In severe weather, when the slaves could not be brought on deck, the mortality was often frightful. An instance is stated of "a schooner, which carried only one hundred and forty slaves, meeting with a gale of wind which lasted eighteen hours, and losing, in that brief space of time, fifty slaves,"—upwards of one-third of the whole number.

But worse misfortunes than storms sometimes overtook these poor wretches. Mr. William James testifies as follows:—"In the year 1779, being master of the Hound, sloop-of-war, and coming from the Bay of Honduras to Jamaica, he fell in, off the Isle of Pines, with two Liverpool Guineamen on the Middle Passage, commanded by Captains Ringmaiden and Jackson, who had very imprudently (but whether wilfully or not he cannot say) missed the island of Jamaica. Captain Nugent gave them chase and came up with them. Mr. James, upon boarding them, found them in great distress, both on account of provisions and water. He asked the captains (for both of them were on board one ship) why they did not go into the watering-place at the

---

* Lords' Report, Part II. Sheet d, 2.

west end of the Isle of Pines (near Cuba). They replied that "they had attempted to get in, but got into shoal water." He then asked them what they intended to have done with their slaves if they had not fallen in with the Hound. They replied, "To make them walk the plank,"—that is, to jump overboard. Mr. James asked them again, why they did not turn a number of the slaves on shore at the Isle of Pines and endeavor to save the rest. They replied, again, "that in such case they could not have recovered the insurance, and that the rest would have gotten on shore."*

The supply of water usually taken appears to have been very scanty. The same witness, speaking of his experience on board the Britannia, says, "Their rooms were so hot and intolerable that they were continually calling out for water, and they generally came upon deck in a sweat. * * * They were served twice a day with water, which is given them in a pannikin of tin, of such dimensions as to hold not quite half a pint."†

Dysentery and diseases of a similar character were common among them. The details, as furnished by eye-witnesses who have given their experience, are too loathsome for reproduction. Mr. Falconbridge, a surgeon in this trade, who published a work on this subject in 1789, after giving a minute description of the scene below, adds, "The deck or floor of their rooms resembled a slaughter-house. It is not in the power of the human imagination to picture to itself a situation more dreadful or disgusting. Numbers of the slaves fainted and were carried on deck, where some of them

* Lords' Report, Part II. Sheet d, 7.
† Report cited, Part II. Sheet d, 7.

5*

died, and the others were with difficulty restored. It
had nearly proved fatal to me also."*

That, under such a system, the average mortality
should be very great, can surprise no one. What the
true average was is somewhat difficult to determine.
That it was chiefly caused by the plan of packing
human beings, sometimes for days and nights together,
in a width of from twelve to sixteen inches each, is
certain. The Rev. John Newton, who in early life had
gone out as mate in a slaver, after stating that on his
first voyage they buried one-third of the number taken,
added that on a subsequent voyage they did not lose
one,—"the only instance of the kind that was ever
known," he admits. Being cross-questioned as to the
probable cause of this exceptional result, he said it was
to be ascribed to the fact that, "with room for two
hundred and twenty slaves, the number for which his
cargo was calculated, they carried ninety only."

The mortality was least from the windward coast,
greatest from Bonny, Calabar, Benin, and Gaboon. Individual instances were frequently adduced by the
witnesses in which it was about five per cent. Occasionally a witness alleges that to be the average; but
this was in the windward trade. From the other points
named, they usually admit an average of ten per cent.
Mr. James Penny, eleven years a slave-captain, speaking of the trade generally, said, "On an average he estimated (from his own experience and the best information he could collect) that the mortality was one-
twelfth."

The only official table on this subject given in the
Lords' Report indicates a much higher rate of mortality than that admitted by these slave-traders. This

* Falconbridge's Account of the Slave-Trade, p. 31.

table is taken from the books of the Board of Trade: it exhibits the number of negroes shipped, and the number delivered, throughout nine years, namely, from 1680 to 1688, both inclusive, by the "African Company," and is from a statement made by the company itself. It is as follows :—

TABLE.

Years.	Negroes shipped.	Negroes delivered.	Yearly loss per cent.	Average loss per cent.
1680.........	5,190	3,751	27¾	
1681.........	6,327	4,989	21¼	
1682.........	6,330	4,494	29	
1683.........	9,081	6,488	28½	
1684.........	5,384	3,845	28½	
1685.........	8,658	6,304	29¾	
1686.........	8,355	6,812	18⅝	
1687.........	5,606	4,777	14⅝	
1688.........	5,852	4,936	15¾	
Total...	60,783	46,394		23⅔

The mortality, it will be observed, was fourteen thousand three hundred and eighty-nine out of sixty thousand seven hundred and eighty-three shipped; that is, *twenty-three and two-thirds per cent.**

The results from an official table like this, presenting an average on so large a scale, are far more reliable than any deductions from isolated cases or individual testimony or opinion. The very witnesses who spoke of five per cent. as the usual loss, when pressed in cross-questioning, admitted far heavier losses to be of frequent occurrence,—as John Newton, Archibald Dalzell, Thomas Eldred. This last admitted that on a

---

* It is worthy of regard, in connection with this excessive mortality, that it occurred among persons all taken in the very prime of life.

single voyage he lost half his slaves and half his crew.

The great crime avenged itself on those who aided in its perpetration. The epidemics which prevailed among the slaves were often communicated to the sailors, exposed as they were on deck day and night, and daily employed in occupations the most infectious and revolting, cleansing the lower decks, and the like.

Sir George Yonge says, " A Guinea-ship seldom returns with more than half her complement of sailors; and he believes the annual loss of seamen in that trade is equal to the manning of two ships-of-the-line."

The celebrated Thomas Clarkson supplied to the Lords' Committee evidence on this point. He submitted a table exhibiting the results as to eighty-eight slavers that returned to Liverpool in the years 1786 and 1787. It showed that out of three thousand one hundred and seventy sailors shipped, there came home but fourteen hundred and twenty-eight.—less than one-half. Six hundred and forty-two (about twenty per cent.) are recorded as having died. The rest had deserted, or were left behind on account of sickness. Of those who returned, many went to the hospital, and never recovered their health.

Another table shows the deaths of seamen on twenty-four West Indiamen, in a single voyage, to have been six; while in twenty-four slavers it was two hundred and sixteen. The average number of seamen employed on slavers being thirty-six on each (as three thousand one hundred and seventy on eighty-eight vessels, in the table just referred to), the above is a mortality of two hundred and sixteen out of eight hundred and sixty-four, or just twenty-five per cent.

Mr. Clarkson shows, by other tables, that the loss of seamen on board slavers is twenty times as great,

in proportion to numbers, as on board vessels in the
Petersburg or Newfoundland or Greenland trade; and
he adds an expression of his belief that "the annual
loss of seamen in English slave-traders is greater than
that in all other English trading-vessels put together."*

So odious did this service become that seamen could
usually be obtained for it only by fraudulent means,—
through crimps and landlords of sailors' boarding-
houses,—though two months' wages (instead of the
usual month's pay) were offered in advance.

Upon the whole, it seems to be sufficiently established that the usual rate of mortality among seamen was not less than twenty-five per cent. for each
voyage,—that is, during one year; for the rule of the
African slave-trade was one round voyage each year.

As to the mortality among the slaves, there seems
no good reason why we should not adopt the rate of
loss shown in the statement of the "African Company" as the average on sixty thousand slaves shipped
in their vessels; namely, *twenty-three and two-thirds per
cent.*

But even to this terrible mortality a material item
may have to be added.

Among the documents in the Lords' Report is a
Report, presented December 12, 1788, by a committee
of the Jamaica House of Assembly to that house.

This committee, desiring to avert the inferences as to
ill treatment of slaves, liable to be drawn from the great
decrease of the slave population of the island, made
inquiry "as to the number of new negroes that have
perished in the harbors of this island between the time
of their being reported at the custom-house and the

---

* Lords of Council Report, Part II. Sheet f, 3.

day of sale,—*all which are reported, in official books and
returns, as negroes actually imported.*" They found, from
the examination of a negro-factor (Mr. Lindo), that
"out of seven thousand eight hundred and seventy-
three negroes consigned to him in the years 1786, 1787,
and 1788, and reported at the custom-house, three hundred and sixty-three died in the harbor of Kingston
before the day of sale."* This gives a mortality of
about *four and two-thirds per cent.* on shipboard after
entry and before landing.

It does not clearly appear from the table of the African Company whether by "negroes delivered" they
mean those entered as arrived in the books of the office,
or those actually offered for sale. If the former, then
we have four and two-thirds per cent. to add to twenty-
three and two-thirds per cent. furnished in the African
Company's table,—making an aggregate of *twenty-eight
and one-third per cent.* as the average mortality incident
to the passage.

What shall we say of the estimates of those slave-
dealers who would have us believe that the entire
average mortality among slaves on the terrible Middle
Passage amounted to but one-fifth of the mortality
among the crews of slavers, and only to about the percentage which, by official documents, we find to have
taken place after the close of the voyage, during a few
days' delay in harbor previous to disembarkation?

On the whole, whether this loss in harbor is to be
added to the African Company's estimate or not, it may
be confidently assumed that the mortality among slaves
imported from the Eastern to the Western hemisphere,
estimated from the time of shipping to that of landing,
did not fall short of from twenty to twenty-five per cent.

* Lords of Council Report, Part III. Sheet R.

Lest we exaggerate, however, let us put it at *twenty per cent.* only.*

It is considered a bloody battle when ten per cent. of the combatants engaged are killed or wounded. The loss at Gettysburg did not amount to so high a percentage. Nor, even when that proportion of killed and wounded is reached, does the ultimate mortality amount to five per cent.

Through what a frightful ordeal, then, were these poor wretches, during their incarceration of eight or ten weeks on board Christian-owned slavers, doomed to pass! Their ranks twice decimated in that brief period; their numbers, without regard to age or sex, thinned by death as the numbers of soldiers passing through four sanguinary battles seldom are; not inspired, as the soldier may be, by zeal in a cause; not sustained, as the soldier in battle is, by hope of victory; their future dark, purposeless, despairing, as the prospect of pitiless slavery, ending only at death, could make it; what people, even under the harrow of pagan victory, were ever made to endure what they endured!

And this crime of one portion of God's creatures against another portion was committed not in the case

---

* It may not be wholly unnecessary to remind the reader, if he be not familiar with the calculation of percentages, that if twenty per cent. of the negroes received on board be the number lost on the Middle Passage, while we must deduct that percentage from the total shipped to ascertain the number landed in the colonies, we must *add, not twenty, but twenty-five per cent.* to the number landed, if we wish to obtain the number shipped. Thus, if the number of negroes shipped be one hundred, we obtain the number landed—namely, eighty—by deducting twenty per cent. from one hundred; but to these eighty we must add twenty-five per cent. on eighty, in order to obtain the original number shipped,—namely, one hundred.

The term Middle Passage is not to be understood as designating the trans-oceanic route to the West Indies from any particular portion of the slave-coast. "*Middle Passage,* or *Mid-passage,* the passage of a slave-ship from Africa across the Atlantic Ocean."— *Worcester's Dictionary.*

of thousands, not even of millions only : it was committed, through the persistent barbarities of three centuries and a half, in the case of tens of millions ! When we consider the character of the means employed in Africa to fill up the slave-cargoes, the wasting wars waged to procure prisoners, the marauding bands of kidnappers firing villages and killing all who resisted, the slaughter of those who were too young, and the abandonment of those who were too old or infirm, to be marketable. the deaths on the long desert-journey, and again in the pestilence-invaded barracoons, and yet again in the dungeons of the slave-ship,—when we reflect upon all these prolific sources of mortality, we shall not be inclined to consider Lord Palmerston guilty of exaggeration when he calculated that we must treble the number of slaves actually landed in the colonies, to find the total of persons who were consigned to death or slavery by the various operations of the trade, from its inception in the Old World to its close in the harbors of the New.

But, lest in this the British Premier should have exaggerated, let us assume that the number of those who perished in Africa by slave-wars, marauding murders, pestilence. and the extremity of hardship previous to embarkation, was but equal to the number embarked ; in other words, let us, to obtain the entire number of victims, lower the estimate to double the number only that were actually received on board slave-ships. Then, according to our previous calculation, assuming the number shipped from Africa in the three and a half centuries through which this traffic lasted to have been fifteen millions and a half, we have thirty-one millions as the total number of negroes who have been consigned to death or to foreign slavery, that one race of men might live by the labor of another.

THIRTY-ONE MILLIONS! a portion of mankind equal in number to the entire inhabitants, Northern and Southern, white and colored, of the United States!

Of these thirty-one millions, upwards of three millions (a population equal to that of the United States when Independence was declared) were cast into the Atlantic;* while less than twelve millions and a half were landed in colonial ports and distributed to planters from the auction-block.†

Never, in any three centuries of man's written history, was the violation of a great principle alike in political economy, in national morals, and in the religion of Christ, followed by a succession of outrages against God's creatures,—in numbers a vast nation,—so openly sanctioned by public law and solemn treaty, so shamelessly countenanced by public opinion, yet so marked at every stage of its progress by those flagrant enormities which usually arouse loud-spoken indignation, even when they do not stir to practical reform, among mankind!

---

* The dead were thrown overboard even in port. Captain Cook, commanding a trading-vessel on the east coast of Africa in 1836, 1837, and 1838, informed Mr. Fowell Buxton that slaves who "die on board, in ports, are never interred on shore, but are invariably thrown overboard, when they sometimes float backwards and forwards with the tide for a week, should the sharks and alligators not devour them."—*The African Slave-Trade*, by Thomas Fowell Buxton, London, 1839, p. 93.

† See, for confirmation of the moderation of these estimates, Appendix, Note A.

CHAPTER VII.

WHAT BECAME OF THE IMPORTED SLAVES.

We have raised the curtain on but the first two acts of the Great Tragedy,—the scene being laid, of the first in Africa, of the second in the prison-slaver. The third and last, opening on colonial plantations, remains to be glanced at. We must say a few words as to the treatment of those who survived death to become, in a foreign land, slaves, and the progenitors of slaves.

The graphic recital of individual barbarities, authentic examples of which can be found without number, are best calculated to stir indignation; but a doubt may obtrude itself, in reading these, as to how far they constitute the rule, and how far they are to be taken as the exception only. Statistical details on a large scale, grave and dispassionate though their language be, addressed not to the heart, but to the reason, carry with them a force of evidence far beyond that of individual example,—a force of evidence against which sophistry strives in vain,—which compels conviction, except when the mind is closed against all proof by the hermetic influence of prejudice.

I select an example of such evidence, based on official tables running through nearly three-quarters of a century, and bearing upon the character of slavery in the principal English colony in the West Indies. The character of England for humanity, as compared with that of other owners of slave-colonies,—Spain, France, Holland,—is not below the average; and, on that score, the example may be assumed as fair.

To the Jamaica House of Assembly, convened by the

governor of the colony, August 6, 1702, a return was made of the negroes and stock then on the island. The number of slaves was forty-one thousand five hundred and ninety-six.*

In the Report of the Lords in Council, from which I have already so copiously extracted, is a table† giving the number of negroes annually imported into, and exported from, the island of Jamaica, from the year 1702 to the year 1775, both inclusive,—that is, during seventy-four years :—

There were imported... 497,736
There were exported 137,014
                                                                         ——————
Leaving an addition, by importation, to the negro popu-
lation of the island, in seventy-four years, of............ 360,722

These two items, of forty-one thousand five hundred and ninety-six negroes in the island in 1702, and of three hundred and sixty thousand seven hundred and twenty-two imported from Africa from that time up to 1775,—together four hundred and two thousand three hundred and eighteen,—give the number of negroes who would have been in the island in 1775, if the population had neither augmented by natural increase, nor diminished by mortality, in the previous seventy-four years.

But, in point of fact, this population of four hundred and two thousand three hundred and eighteen was represented in 1775 by only one hundred and ninety-two thousand seven hundred and eighty-seven survivors.‡ It had diminished in three-quarters of a cen-

---

* Annals of Jamaica, by the Rev. G. W. Bridges, A.M., London, 1827, vol. i. p. 331.

† Lords of Council Report, Part III., Jamaica, Sheet P.

‡ The Rev. Mr. Bridges, after quoting the table above given and stating that, after deducting the negroes exported from those imported, three hun-

tury by two hundred and nine thousand five hundred and thirty-one,—that is, to less than one-half.

A similar table to that above referred to for Jamaica is given for the British West Indian colony next in importance, namely, the island of Barbadoes. It extends, however, over seventeen years only, namely, from 1764 to 1780, both inclusive.* It indicates a rate of decrease in the slave population far greater even than that in Jamaica.

It appears from the table that in 1764 there were in the island seventy thousand seven hundred and six negroes,—that there were imported in the next seventeen years, namely, up to 1780, thirty-eight thousand eight hundred and forty-three; no importations of negroes in the last seven years of the period, nor any exportations of them throughout the period, being recorded.

To seventy thousand seven hundred and six (the number in 1764) add thirty-eight thousand eight hundred and forty-three (the number imported in seventeen years), and we have one hundred and nine thousand five hundred and forty-nine as the number of negroes who, if there had been no natural increase or decrease of population, would have been alive in 1780. But in that year there were but sixty-eight thousand two hundred and seventy alive on the island.

---

dred and sixty thousand seven hundred and twenty-two were left for the supply of the island, adds that the number alive in 1775 was one hundred and ninety-two thousand seven hundred and eighty-seven.—*Work cited*, vol. ii. p. 456.

A resident for years in Jamaica, Mr. Bridges had access, through the Duke of Manchester, governor of the island, to all important official documents. An apologist of slavery, he may be trusted as to any evidence against it.

* Lords of Council Report, Part III., Barbadoes, Table A, No. 15.

At this rate of decrease, the population *would have diminished to one-half in twenty-three years.*

But to obtain general results we must look to more comprehensive estimates than these.

Unfortunately, there are to be found no full statistical details which might enable us to calculate, with accuracy, the number of negroes and their descendants of mixed blood now on the Western Hemisphere. We know that there were, in 1860, four millions four hundred and thirty-five thousand seven hundred and nine in the United States.*

We know that in the West Indies, including Guiana, there were emancipated by England, France, Denmark, Sweden, and Holland, about nine hundred and fifteen thousand slaves,† and the usual estimate is, that to these should be added one-fifth to obtain the present colored

---

* Preliminary Report of Eighth Census, p. 7.

† The total number emancipated was as follows:—

By England	770,390
" France	248,560
" Holland	45,000
" Denmark	27,144
" Sweden	531
Total	1,091,625

But of the slaves emancipated by England one hundred and two thousand three hundred and sixty-three were not in the Western Hemisphere,—namely, at the Cape thirty-five thousand seven hundred, and in the Mauritius sixty-six thousand six hundred and thirteen. There were also among those liberated by France seventy-four thousand five hundred and one in the Eastern Hemisphere,—namely, in the island of Bourbon sixty thousand six hundred and fifty-one, in Senegal ten thousand three hundred and fifty, and in Nossi-bé three thousand five hundred. Deducting these two items of one hundred and two thousand three hundred and sixty-three, and seventy-four thousand five hundred and one, from one million ninety-one thousand six hundred and twenty-five, we have nine hundred and fourteen thousand six hundred and sixty-one as the total of slaves emancipated in the West Indies, including Guiana.

population of these colonies.   This would give one million and ninety-eight thousand—or say, in round numbers, one million one hundred thousand—as the entire
colored population of the West Indian colonies of
England, France, Holland, Denmark, and Sweden,* let
us say in 1860.

The census-returns of the Spanish West Indian colonies, still slave, are imperfect; and the several estimates
of population in these islands vary widely.   The most
authentic estimates, based on actual census-returns,
make the slave and free colored population of Cuba, as
late as 1853, a little more than half a million.†   With

---

* This is, probably, a full estimate.   There were freed in Jamaica three
hundred and eleven thousand and seventy slaves,—one-third of the whole
number emancipated in the West Indies.   But by the census of 1844 the
total black and colored population of the island was but three hundred
and sixty-one thousand six hundred and fifty-seven, having diminished
in ten years nearly twenty thousand.   Sewell (Ordeal of Free Labor in
the British West Indies, New York, 1862, p. 245) says, "If the estimate
of mortality by cholera and small-pox within a few years be correct, I do
not believe, after making every allowance for a proper increase by birth,
that the black and colored population of Jamaica exceeds at the present
day three hundred and fifty thousand."   This is but *twelve* per cent. more
than the number of slaves freed.

If Cochin's estimate of the population of the West Indies be correct,
there were in the British West Indian colonies, in 1855, but eight hundred
and forty-five thousand, of whom between one hundred and forty thousand
and one hundred and fifty thousand were whites,—leaving say seven hundred thousand for the entire colored population.   (Cochin, tom. i. p. 478
and pp. 366, 367.)   But England emancipated in the West Indies six
hundred and seventy thousand slaves (Cochin, tom. i. p. 367), or within
thirty thousand as many as comprised, in 1855 (according to Cochin's
estimate), the entire colored population in her West Indian colonies.

The addition to the number of slaves emancipated in the West Indies
of one-fifth, or twenty per cent., to make up the total colored population,
say in 1860, is evidently ample.

† I take these from a work published in 1855, entitled "Cuba," from the
Spanish of Don J. M. de la Torre, edited by R. S. Fisher, statistical editor
of Colton's works.   A table (p. 119) gives census-returns at intervals from
1775.   The three last are—

a fair allowance for increase since that date, we may put it in 1860 at five hundred and thirty thousand.

Porto Rico, a flourishing and increasing colony, contained, by a census-return of 1846,* four hundred and forty-seven thousand nine hundred and fourteen inhabitants, of whom about fifty-four per cent. were white, leaving about two hundred and six thousand colored. The rate of increase for the sixteen years preceding was a little upwards of two per cent. a year. As but fifty or fifty-five thousand of the colored people in this island are slaves, so that the gradual falling off of the slave-trade would not very seriously affect the population, we may suppose that some twenty-five per cent. (say fifty-one thousand five hundred) have been added since,—making, in all, two hundred and fifty-seven thousand five hundred for the entire colored population of Porto Rico.

	White.	Free Colored and Black.	Slaves.	Total.
In 1846............	425,767	149,226	323,759	898,752
In 1849............	457,133	164,410	323,897	945,440
In 1853............	501,988	176,647	330,425	1,009,060

In 1846 there were four hundred and seventy-two thousand nine hundred and eighty-two free and slave; in 1853 there were five hundred and seven thousand and seventy-two,—an increase in seven years of about thirty-four thousand. If (as the supplies from the slave-trade have been diminished) we put the increase since then at forty-three thousand, we shall have five hundred and fifty thousand as the present total.

* "Porto Rico," by J. T. O'Neil, edited by R. S. Fisher, 1855, has returns from an early date. The three last are—

In 1830..	330,051
In 1834..	358,836
In 1846..	447,914

In the census of 1834, the whites were fifty-four per cent. of the whole population, the free colored being thirty-five per cent., and the slaves eleven per cent.

This would give in the Spanish West Indian colonies a colored population, in 1860, of seven hundred and eighty-seven thousand five hundred.

I have not been able to find any official returns of the population of Hayti later than 1826. In 1820, in a "Mémoire sur Saint-Dominique," by Lieutenant-General Baron Pamphile de Lacroix, the population of the island is put at five hundred and one thousand, of whom only one thousand are set down as white.* In 1825, M. Placide Justin estimated the population at seven hundred thousand.† But in 1826, Charles Mackenzie, British Consul-General in Hayti, obtained an official population-return, not published, which had recently been made to the Haytien Chamber of Commerce. It gives the population of each commune separately, making the total population of the island, at that time, four hundred and twenty-three thousand and forty-two.‡ This return Mr. Mackenzie considers more reliable than any other. It affords proof how little trustworthy are vague estimates of population, which usually overrun the truth, in consequence, probably, of the de-

---

* The proportion of slaves at this time is said to be nine per cent. only. The estimate is—

Blacks	480,000
Mulattoes	20,000
Whites	1,000
Total	501,000

† Notes on Hayti, by Charles Mackenzie, F. R. S., London, 1830. vol. ii. p. 112.

‡ Notes on Hayti, above cited, vol. ii. pp. 113, 114.

The population is thus divided:—

Population of the Northwest and South (late French part of the island)	351,819
Population of the East (Spanish part)	71,223
Total	423,042

sire of a nation or its Government, in the absence of an undeniable census, to represent its numerical strength as great as possible.

Some very partial returns of an authentic character, furnished by Mackenzie,* give the rate of natural increase in the population in certain communes at about three-quarters of one per cent. only per annum. But no trustworthy deductions can be made from returns so limited. The actual rate of increase from 1836 to 1860—thirty-four years—is probably double this, say one and a half per cent. a year.

Allowing for omissions,† and for Mackenzie's opinion, that the census given, though the most reliable document he could obtain, may be an under-estimate,‡ let us, instead of the total of four hundred and twenty-three thousand and forty-two there given as the population in 1826, assume the black and colored population of Hayti in 1826 at Baron de Lacroix's estimate of five hundred thousand, adding thereto, to bring it up to 1860, one and a half per cent. a year for thirty-four years,—that is, fifty-one per cent.,—and we have the total negro and mulatto population of the island at seven hundred and fifty-five thousand.§

---

* These returns show an annual excess of births over deaths of eighty, on an average of five years, in the commune of St. Jago, containing eleven thousand and fifty-six inhabitants; and, again, a similar excess of seventy-five per annum, on an average of six years, in the commune of Cape Haytien, on twelve thousand one hundred and fifty-one inhabitants: in neither case reaching three-quarters of one per cent.—*Notes on Haiti*, vol. ii. pp. 117 and 119.

† Grands Bois, the residence of the Maroons, or refugee negroes, then inhabiting the mountains which stretch from the neighborhood of Mirebalais to the coast on the east of Jacmel, is omitted, as that wandering people could not be reached so as to enumerate them. Their number at that time is commonly estimated at six thousand.

‡ Notes on Haiti, vol. ii. p. 116.

§ Victor Schölcher, who, in 1842, published "Les Colonies Françaises,"

As respects Central and South America, any estimate of the number of negroes and their descendants
of mixed blood must be founded on data still more
uncertain than those which relate to the West Indies.
Not only are we without any census of modern date
to aid in the research, but an element of uncertainty
intervenes which even census-returns would fail to
dispel. The aboriginal Indian races and their descendants of mixed blood are in large proportion all
over this country, and are so blended in some portions
of it that it is impossible to distinguish between them
and the African mulatto of various shades.

---

is the author of two volumes, published in 1843, entitled "Colonies
Etrangères et Haiti." The spirit in which his works are written may be
judged from the motto, " It would be as easy to regulate humanely as-
sassination as slavery;" and his opinions on Hayti are entitled to the
more weight as they are the result of a personal visit to that island, and
exploration of its interior. He says:—

"There has been no census taken for the last fifteen years. * * *
Though children swarm in the cabins, those who speak in good faith concur in the admission that the population does not increase. The government, indeed, puts the population at eight hundred thousand; but the
general opinion is that it does not exceed seven hundred thousand."—
Colonies Etrangères et Haiti, vol. ii. pp. 264, 265.

This is the judgment of one whose book is a defence of the Haytiens
and of their character, and who is evidently disposed to represent every
thing as favorably as truth will warrant.

Colton's Descriptive Atlas (1863) gives the entire population of the
island in 1860 at seven hundred and eight thousand five hundred. Some
others put it as high as from eight hundred thousand to nine hundred
thousand. Upon the whole, the data here brought together induce
me to believe that these latter figures, like the government estimate to
which Schölcher alludes, are an exaggeration, and that, in estimating
the colored population of the island in 1860 at seven hundred and fifty-
five thousand, we are as likely to exceed the actual amount as to fall
short of it. The number of whites in the island are scarcely worth
reckoning.

Diligent search has convinced me that reliable documents as to the
actual population of this island are not to be obtained.

Brazil, the only considerable portion of the South American continent in which slavery exists, contains, of course, by far the larger number of negroes,—probably four-fifths, or more, of all that are to be found in Central or South America. Into this country slaves were imported from Africa, in considerable numbers, as late as fifteen years ago.*

A census, spoken of as official, bearing date June 22, 1831, states the entire population at five millions thirty-five thousand, of which two millions are set down as slaves.† The free colored population is not given.

An estimate in the Penny Cyclopædia puts the negro population, in 1836, at two millions; namely, sixteen hundred thousand slaves and four hundred thousand free.‡ If the proportion here given between slave and free be correct, and if the census of 1831 may be trusted, the number of free colored of African descent was then five hundred thousand. This would make the entire colored population of African descent, in 1831, two millions five hundred thousand; that is, about one-half of the whole population, the other half being whites, Indians, and a mixed race sharing the Indian blood.

From the year 1831 to the year 1856 we find no record of any population-returns claiming to be offi-

---

* M. de Souza, Brazilian Minister of Foreign Affairs, stated, under date May 14, 1853, that the number of slaves imported was—

In 1846	50,324
In 1847	56,172
In 1848	60,000
In 1849	54,000

He added that in 1852 the number imported had been reduced to seven hundred.—*Cochin*, tom. ii. p. 238.

† Horner's Brazil and Uruguay, p. 71.

‡ Penny Cyclopædia, Vol. V., art. Brazil.

cial. In 1856 the Brazilian Government published returns, summing up seven millions six hundred and seventy-eight thousand, but not distinguishing the races.

The latest, and probably the most reliable, authority on this subject is the work of Kidder and Fletcher on Brazil, from which (page 612) the above returns are taken.* These gentlemen believe the government returns of 1856 to be an over-estimate; and they give, as more trustworthy, a table made up from the estimates of Sr. Francisco Nunes de Souza, a native statistician, quoted also by Ewbank. The table was published in the "Agricultor Brazileiro." It is for 1856, and sums up seven millions and forty thousand.†

---

* Kidder and Fletcher inform us, in their preface, that their "experience in the Brazilian Empire embraces a period of twenty years;" and they add, "the authors have consulted every important work in French, German, English, and Portuguese that could throw light on the history of Brazil, and likewise various published Memoirs and Discourses read before the flourishing Geographical and Historical Society at Rio de Janeiro. For statistics they have either personally examined the imperial and provincial archives, or have quoted directly from Brazilian state papers."—*Brazil and the Brazilians*, Preface, pp. 4, 5.

† In the province of Amazonas	30,000
" " Pará	190,000
" " Maranhão	280,000
" " Piauhy	170,000
" " Ceará	350,000
" " Rio Grande do Norte	160,000
" " Parahiba	230,000
" " Pernambuco	800,000
" " Alagôas	210.000
" " Sergipe	180,000
" " Bahia	880,000
" " Espirito Santo	60,000
" " Rio de Janeiro	1,400,000
" " S. Paulo	680,000
Carried forward	5,620,000

The same authors give us also estimates of the percentage of slaves to the free population in one-half of the provinces composing the empire. It is to be regretted that the proportion in the other half, the most populous, containing more than three-fifths of the population, cannot be obtained. These estimates, we are told, are "from the very careful computations of the Hon. J. U. Petit, formerly United States Consul at Maranham." They show an aggregate of nine hundred and forty-four thousand six hundred and twenty-three slaves in a population of two millions six hundred and eighty thousand.* The number of free colored is not given.

		Brought forward......	5,620,000
In the province of	Paraná..		70,000
"	"	Santa Catharina........................	90,000
"	"	Rio Grande..............................	240,000
"	"	Minas Geraes...........................	800,000
"	"	Goyaz	120,000
"	"	Mato Grosso..............................	100,000
		Total population of Brazil.......................	7,040,000

From Brazil and the Brazilians, already cited, p. 599.

* The details are as follows:—

Total Population.		Slave population to free in the proportion of	Number of Slaves.
Pará	190,000	1 to 1.431	78,157
Piauhy......................................	170,000	1 to 2.666	46,372
Rio Grande do Norte..............	160,000	1 to 7.221	19,162
Alagôas.....................................	210,000	1 to 4.221	40,222
Sergipe.....................................	180,000	1 to 2.927	45,836
Espirito Santo.........................	60,000	1 to 2.009	19,940
Rio de Janeiro.........................	1,400,000	1 to 1.181	641,907
Santa Catharina......................	90,000	1 to .5	15,000
Goyaz..	120,000	1 to .7	15,000
Mato Grosso.............................	100,000	1 to 3.4	22,727
	2,680,000	Total slaves.....	944,623

From Brazil and the Brazilians, p. 599.

To bring these estimates up to 1860, we must add the increase of population during four years. The rate of increase, deduced from the average of estimates going back thirty years, is about one and three-quarters per cent. a year, or seven per cent. in four years. This gives us four hundred and ninety-two thousand eight hundred, which, added to seven millions forty thousand, raises the total population of Brazil, in 1860, to seven millions five hundred and thirty-two thousand eight hundred,—an estimate which, in default of an official census, we adopt. It is somewhat above the average of the current estimates of the day.*

If the proportion of slaves to free persons be the same in the remaining ten provinces as in those estimated, then the total number of slaves in the empire

---

* Of popular estimates, found in modern gazetteers and descriptive atlases, a few are a little above this, while others are considerably below it. The average of these would make the population, in 1860, about seven millions and a quarter only.

The Imperial Gazetteer puts the total, in 1854, at six millions sixty-five thousand; Harper's Gazetteer, in 1855, at six millions one hundred and fifty thousand. Passing by McCulloch's Gazetteer, where it is "vaguely estimated at five millions," we have the estimate in Mitchell's Descriptive Atlas of seven millions seven hundred thousand as the population in 1860. Colton puts it, for the same year, at seven millions seven hundred and eighty thousand.

Adding to the two first estimates at the rate of one and three-quarters per cent. a year to bring them up to 1860, we have six millions seven hundred and one thousand three hundred, six millions six hundred and eighty-eight thousand one hundred and thirty, seven millions seven hundred thousand, and seven millions seven hundred and eighty-seven thousand, as various estimates of the population in 1860. Averaging these, we have seven millions two hundred and nineteen thousand one hundred and seven as the total population of Brazil.

We are of opinion, however, that the estimate we have adopted, based on the calculations of M. de Souza and endorsed by Messrs. Kidder and Fletcher, and which exceeds the above by three hundred and twenty-three thousand, is more reliable, and probably approaches nearly the truth.

of Brazil was, in the year 1860, two millions six hundred and fifty-five thousand.

But, inasmuch as the largest proportions of slaves to free persons are to be found in the populous provinces on the Atlantic coast, and as three of these, to wit, Pernambuco, Bahia, and Minas Geraes, each with a population of eight hundred thousand or upwards, are among the provinces not estimated, we think the above total of two millions six hundred and fifty-five thousand slaves is probably somewhat too low, and that it may bear an addition of ten per cent. This would give for the empire of Brazil, in 1860, two millions nine hundred and twenty thousand five hundred slaves,—an estimate which we believe to be as near the truth as any thing we are likely to obtain.*

I find no reliable data in regard to the number of free persons of African descent, of which the probable reason is the great mixture of colored races. The aborigines of Brazil at the period of its conquest are said to have numbered between four and five millions,† and though, probably, not more than a fifth of that number now survive, the half and quarter breeds are very numerous.

Ewbank gives an estimate by Senhor de Souza (the same writer, probably, whose calculation of later date is relied on by Kidder and Fletcher), in which, putting the total at about the same I have given,‡ he divides

---

* Cochin, accurate as he usually is, undoubtedly understates the number of slaves in Brazil. Writing in 1861, he says, in one place, "More than two millions," and in another he assumes two millions as the number. "Près de 4,000,000 esclaves aux Etats-Unis, plus de 2,000,000 au Brésil" is his expression. And again, "Les 2,000,000 Africains, esclaves au Brésil." —*Cochin*, vol. ii. p. 237.

† Life in Brazil, by Thomas Ewbank, 1856, p. 430.

‡ The exact figures are seven millions three hundred and sixty thousand, and the date appears to be 1845. This is but forty thousand less

the population into two millions one hundred and sixty thousand whites, three millions one hundred and twenty thousand negro slaves, eight hundred thousand domesticated Indians,* one hundred and eighty thousand free blacks, and one million one hundred thousand "free colored." Unless all the Indian half and quarter breeds are included in the class of "domesticated Indians," which is not likely, we cannot regard the "free colored" as all of African blood.

On the other hand, it is certain that the number of free negroes and mulattoes in Brazil is large,—larger, probably, than in any other slave country. "By the Brazilian laws, a slave can go before a magistrate, have his price fixed, and can purchase himself."† Large numbers avail themselves of this privilege, and the class of freemen is rapidly increasing. All writers agree that more than half the population of Brazil consists of persons of African descent, slave and free.

Under these circumstances, as it is my object not to overstate the case, and therefore to avoid all under-

---

than his subsequent estimate for 1856. Ewbank says, "Nothing like positive data was within this writer's reach." From De Souza's last calculation we may infer that he found his estimate for 1845 too high.

* A report by Councillor Vellosa, made in 1819 (quoted by Ewbank, work cited, p. 430), giving the total population at four millions three hundred and ninety-six thousand three hundred and twenty-one, includes "eight hundred thousand wild Indians."

† Brazil and the Brazilians, p. 133. The author adds, "Some of the most intelligent men that I met with in Brazil—educated at Paris and Coimbra—were of African descent,—men whose ancestors were slaves. Some of the closest students in the National Library are mulattoes. The largest and most successful printing establishment in Rio—that of Sr. F. Paulo Brito—is owned and directed by a mulatto. In the colleges, the medical, law, and theological schools, there is no distinction of color. * * * I was informed that a man of mental endowments, even if he had been a slave, would be debarred from no official station, however high, unless it might be that of Imperial Senator."

estimates of the number of negroes who have survived
the horrors of the Middle Passage and the cruelties
of slavery, I assume De Souza's figures without any
deduction for Indian blood,—making the free negro
population of all shades one million two hundred and
eighty thousand.

This, added to the slaves, gives us as the population,
free and slave, of African descent, in the empire of
Brazil, for the year 1860, a total of four millions two
hundred thousand five hundred; leaving less than
three millions and a third for whites, Indians, and Indian mixed races.

One item still remains,—the most vague and uncertain of any,—the number of negroes and mulattoes in
the free republics of Central and South America. In
all of these the aboriginal races and their descendants
vastly predominate. In all of them the mixture of
race and gradations of color defy analysis. In none
of them has slavery had more than a comparatively
ephemeral existence. But, as negroes do not voluntarily emigrate to the Western Hemisphere, all the
negroes or mulattoes to be found in these countries
must be originally due to the slave-trade, with such
trifling additions as the straying off of slaves or of free
colored persons from the West Indies, or from Brazil,
may occasionally have made.

In Mexico the number of negroes seems to be accurately ascertained. The various estimates differ but a
few hundreds; none under six thousand and none over
seven thousand.* Let us assume the latter number as
the negro population of Mexico in 1860.

* Albert M. Gilliam, late United States Consul to California, in his
"Travels over the Table-Lands and Cordilleras of Mexico," 1846 (page
164), says, "The census of the population of Mexico, it is said, cannot bo
accurately taken. From the various estimates made by those having the

In Central America, as in Mexico, the representatives of the African race are a very insignificant part of the population.   Squier, formerly Chargé d'Affaires of the United States to the Republics of Central America, is undoubtedly one of the best, if not the very best, authority on that point.   He says, "The population of Central America, in the absence of reliable data, can be calculated only approximately. * * * The following table probably exhibits very nearly the exact proportions in Central America, so far as they may be deduced from existing data and from personal observation :—*

"Whites	100,000
"Indians	1,109,000
"Mixed races	800,000
"Negroes	10,000
"Total	2,019,000."

This would give us, for Mexico and Central Ame-

---

best opportunities of knowing, a table was furnished me by a gentleman who, from his long residence in the country and by some attention paid to the subject, may be relied on as measurably correct."

The table is as follows :—

Indians	4,500,000
Other castes	3,000,000
Negroes	6,000
Total	7,506,000

Brantz Mayer, formerly Secretary of Legation to Mexico, in his work entitled "Mexico; Aztec, Spanish, and Republican," 1853 (vol. ii. page 43), estimates the different classes of the population thus :—

Indians	4,354,886
Whites	1,110,000
Mestizos	2,165,345
Negroes	6,600
Total	7,636,831

* Squier's Notes on Central America, pp. 53, 54.

rica, seventeen thousand. Let us say, in round numbers, twenty thousand.

If we pass to South America, we find in Venezuela —a country coterminous with the slave-colonies of Guiana—a considerable number of negroes. Bonnycastle estimated, in 1818, that there were fifty-four thousand negroes in Venezuela.* Codazzi puts down, in 1841, forty-nine thousand seven hundred and eighty-two slaves.† Negroes were employed in the wars of this republic, and in these many are said to have perished.‡ It is certain that they have not increased in late years. Bonnycastle's calculation for 1818 is probably a full estimate for 1860. But we have put the number at sixty thousand.

New Granada appears to contain a larger number of negroes than any other of the South American republics. Cobb, in his "Historical Sketches of Slavery," puts the total, in 1853, at eighty thousand.§ Bollaert —apparently one of the most reliable authorities, so far as his researches extend—estimates that, in 1860, there were of the Ethiopian race in New Granada eighty thousand.‖ Colton, in his Descriptive Atlas, 1860, apparently following these authorities, puts the population at two millions two hundred and forty-three thousand and fifty-four, of whom eighty thousand were negroes. I shall assume that to be the number.

In Ecquador the number is small. Bollaert sets it down, for the year 1860, at seven thousand eight hun-

---

* Bonnycastle's Spanish America, vol. ii. p. 319.

† Codazzi's Geografia de Venezuela, 1841, p. 241.

‡ Colombia: its Present State, &c., by Col. Francis Hall, Hydrographer in the service of Colombia, p. 15.

§ Historical Sketches of Slavery, 1858, pp. 206, 207.

‖ Antiquarian, Ethnological, and other Researches in New Granada, Ecquador, Peru, and Chili, by W. Bollaert, 1860, p. 7.

dred and thirty-one;* and Colton has the same estimate.

In Peru the largest proportion of negroes is to be
found in the province of Lima. Hill estimates, for the
province, seven thousand five hundred;† Dr. Von
Tschudi puts the slaves, in 1847, in the same province,
at four thousand seven hundred and ninety-two.‡ Bollaert estimates the total negroes in Peru at forty thousand.§ I cannot find, after much search, any estimate
that seems more reliable than this last.

In Chili there have never been more than a few
negroes, either free or slave. The usual remark of the
traveller (as Cobb, Schmidtmeyer, Mollina, and others)
is that very few negroes are to be found there. Bollaert puts the number at thirty-one only; but this must
be an error; for in 1825 slavery was abolished, without
difficulty or disturbance, it is true, which would indicate
that the number was small,—but it is not likely that so
small a number as Bollaert's estimate indicates would
be made the subject of legislation at all. I have put
down for Chili one thousand, which will probably cover
all that are to be found there at this time.

In Bolivia, in a population chiefly Indian, amounting to about two millions, we have no estimate whatever. "Few pure Africans," says Colton. "Some few
Africans," says Bollaert. Probably three thousand
may cover the total amount.

In the Argentine Confederation, previous to the

---

* Work cited, p. 94.

† Travels in Peru and Mexico, 1860, vol. ii. p. 88.

‡ Travels in Peru, 1838–42, Dr. J. J. Von Tschudi, 1847, p. 64.
Of the above 4792, he says 2186 were males, and 3606 females. The
negro population of Peru does not appear to have been due directly to the
slave-trade.

§ Antiquarian, Ethnological, and other Researches in New Granada,
Ecquador, Peru, and Chili, by W. Bollaert, 1860, p. 115.

revolution of July 9, 1816, slavery prevailed, and many slaves had been imported, some directly to Buenos Ayres, others through Brazil. At the present time, the negroes in La Plata are not numerous. There are a good many in Mendoza. The great mass of the population, however, are Indians. If we put the total number of negroes within the Confederation at twenty-five thousand, we shall probably be above rather than below the truth.

In Paraguay there are few negroes to be found.* Five thousand will, I believe, cover the amount.

They are more numerous in Uruguay. To this republic, previous to 1842, about which time slavery was abolished, there had been brought negroes both directly from Africa and also through Southern Brazil. One writer estimates the number of negroes in Uruguay at twenty thousand;† and, as I find in the various works on this country no other estimate, I adopt this.

In Patagonia it would appear, from the various authorities, that no negroes are to be found.

Thus we have, for Mexico, Central America, and South America, apart from Brazil, the following estimate :—

Mexico and Central America	20,000
Venezuela	60,000
New Granada	80,000
Ecquador	7,831
Peru	40,000
Chili	1,000
Bolivia	5,000
Argentine Confederation	25,000
Paraguay	5,000
Uruguay	20,000
Total	263,831

* Histoire du Paraguay, par Demersey, 1860, tome i. p. 374: "Quelques nègres, en très-petit nombre."

† Medical Topography of Brazil and Uruguay, by G. R. B. Horner, Surgeon, U. S. A., p. 184.

Bringing together these various results, we find an approximating estimate of the number of negroes and their descendants on the Western Continent, in the following table:—

Number of Negroes and their descendants in the Western Hemisphere in the year 1860.

In the United States......	4,435,709
In the English, French, Dutch, Danish, and Swedish West Indies, including Guiana......	1,100,000
In the Spanish West Indies......	787,500
In the Island of Hayti......	755,000
In the Empire of Brazil......	4,200,500
In the rest of South America and in Central America......	263,831
In Canada......	20,000
Total......	11,562,540

The total somewhat exceeds eleven millions and a half. But seeing that, after diligent search,* I have been compelled to make up these estimates, especially for South America, from scanty materials, and desiring to put forth no argument founded on exaggerated data, and therefore not to under-estimate the remnant remaining alive, as descendants and representatives of the negroes brought to America from Africa, I add a quarter of a million to the sum of my estimate, and will assume the number of negroes and their descendants in the Western Hemisphere, in 1860, to have been *eleven millions eight hundred and twelve thousand five hundred and forty souls.* This is, beyond question, not an under-estimate of the actual number left.

What is the conclusion, then, at which we are forced to arrive?

The fifteen millions and a half of poor wretches who

---

* For the statistics of the negro population of South America alone, I have examined upwards of a hundred and fifty volumes.

were sentenced by the slave-trade to transportation and slavery in foreign lands, are now, after three centuries of servitude, represented, in these lands, by less than four-fifths of their original number.

When we consider the tendency to natural increase, in human beings, which has gradually swelled the population of the world to its eight hundred or a thousand millions, the above statement. as its stands, must be confessed to embody a terrible condemnation of that system which. as to a population half as large as that of the United States, not only arrested, for eight or ten generations of men, the operation of one of the great laws of the world, but—without the life-destruction of war,* without the deadly agencies of pestilence or famine,—not. as we sometimes express it, by the visitation of God, but by the sole operation of man's crime and the misery thence resulting—produced a retrogression of numbers at a ratio which, had it spread over the habitable earth, would have extinguished, in a few centuries, all human existence.

But the matter has been very imperfectly presented yet. The actual results were far more fatal than the simple statement we have given serves to indicate. To obtain an accurate and intelligible view of these results, we must separate the fifteen millions and a half of expatriated Africans into two portions, and trace out the separate destiny of each.

---

* There was, indeed, the war in Hayti which terminated, in 1804, in independence. But the loss of life consequent thereon has been far more than made up by the natural increase of the population of Hayti since it became free. Humboldt calculated the population, in 1802, at three hundred and fifty thousand ; and after the death of Dessalines, the first emperor, it was rated at four hundred thousand.—*Notes on Haiti,* heretofore cited, vol. ii. p. 110. It has since nearly doubled.

CHAPTER VIII.

STRANGELY CONTRASTING FATE OF THE TWO DIVERGING STREAMS.

MORE than a third of the present representatives of these fifteen millions and a half inhabit, it will be observed, the United States. Less than two-thirds are scattered over the West Indies, Central and South America.

But what proportion, let us inquire, of the negroes shipped in slavers from Africa were the progenitors of the present colored population of the United States, and what proportion went to the West Indies and to Southern America?

Here, as in previous calculations, though the materials be insufficient for absolute accuracy, we can approximate the truth.

In the Report of the Lords of Council, so often already referred to, there is but one table bearing on the subject.* It exhibits the exportation of negroes from the West Indies (then the principal place of their deposit and sale) for five years, namely, from 1783 to 1787, both inclusive,—showing that, in these five years, out of twenty thousand seven hundred and seventy-three negroes exported to all parts, thirteen hundred and ninety-two went to the "States of America;" that is, only about one-fifteenth of the whole,—or two hundred and seventy-eight annually.

Since so small a proportion out of the whole export was directed to the United States, it is evident that

---

* Lords of Council Report, Part IV. Table No. 4.

the demand for slaves at that time could not have been great. Nor do we find, throughout the Report, any allusion to a direct trade by slavers from the African coast to the Continental colonies. Of course it existed, but evidently not to a large extent. The public opinion, as well as the legislation, of the colonies had uniformly been against it.*

---

* The agency of the British Government in fastening slavery upon the Continental colonies is well known. Bancroft has placed it distinctly on record:—

"The inhabitants of Virginia were controlled by the central authority on a subject of vital importance to themselves and their posterity. Their halls of legislation had resounded with eloquence directed against the terrible plague of negro slavery. Again and again they had passed laws restraining the importation of negroes from Africa; but their laws were disallowed. How to prevent them from protecting themselves against the increase of the overwhelming evil was debated by the King in Council, and on the 10th day of December, 1770, he issued an instruction, under his own hand, commanding the governor, 'under pain of the highest displeasure, to assent to no law by which the importation of slaves should be, in any respect, prohibited or obstructed.' In April, 1772, this rigorous order was solemnly debated in the Assembly of Virginia. They were very anxious for an Act to restrain the introduction of people the number of whom already in the colony gave them just cause to apprehend the most dangerous consequences. * * * Virginia resolved to address the King himself, who in Council had cruelly compelled the toleration of the nefarious traffic. They pleaded with him for leave to protect themselves against the nefarious traffic, and these were the words:—

"'The importation of slaves into the colonies from the coast of Africa hath long been considered as a trade of great inhumanity, and, under its present encouragement, we have too much reason to fear, will endanger the very existence of your Majesty's American dominions. We are sensible that some of your Majesty's subjects in Great Britain may reap emolument from this sort of traffic; but, when we consider that it greatly retards the settlement of the colonies with more useful inhabitants, and may, in time, have the most destructive influence, we presume to hope that the interest of a few will be disregarded when placed in competition with the security and happiness of such numbers of your Majesty's dutiful and loyal subjects.

"'Deeply impressed with these sentiments, we most humbly beseech your Majesty to remove all those restraints on your Majesty's governors

"The English Continental colonies," says Bancroft, "were, in the aggregate, always opposed to the African slave-trade. Maryland, Virginia, even Carolina, alarmed at the excessive production, and consequent low price, of their staples, at the heavy debts incurred by the purchase of slaves on credit, and at the dangerous increase of the colored population, each showed an anxious preference for the introduction of white men; and laws designed to restrict importations of slaves are scattered copiously along the records of colonial legislation. The first Continental Congress which took to itself powers of legislation gave a legal expression to the well-formed opinion of the country by resolving (April 6, 1776) that 'no slaves be imported into any of the thirteen United Colonies.' "*

of this colony which inhibit their assenting to such laws as might check so very pernicious a commerce.'

"In this manner Virginia led the host who alike condemned slavery and opposed the slave-trade. Thousands in Maryland and in New Jersey were ready to adopt a similar petition; so were the Legislatures of North Carolina, of Pennsylvania, of New York. Massachusetts, in its towns and in its Legislature, unceasingly combated the condition, as well as the sale, of slaves. There was no jealousy among one another in the strife against the crying evil; Virginia harmonized all opinions, and represented the moral sentiment and policy of them all. When her prayer reached England, Franklin, through the press, called to it the sympathy of the people. Again and again it was pressed upon the attention of the Ministers. But the Government of that day was less liberal than the tribunals; and, while a question respecting a negro from Virginia led the courts of law to an axiom that as soon as any slave sets his foot on English ground he becomes free, the King of England stood in the path of humanity, and made himself the pillar of the slave-trade. Wherever in the colonies a disposition was shown for its restraint, his servants were peremptorily ordered to maintain it without abatement."—*Bancroft's History of the United States*, vol. vi. pp. 413, 414, 415.

In the entire history of Great Britain there is scarcely a more disgraceful page.

* Bancroft's United States, vol. iii. p. 411.

As to the number of slaves actually imported during colonial days, the same historian says:—

"It is not easy to conjecture how many negroes were imported into the English Continental colonies. The usual estimates far exceed the truth. Climate came in aid of opinion to oppose the introduction of them. * * * From the first they appear to have increased,—though, owing to the inequality of the sexes, not rapidly in the first generation. Previous to the year 1740, there may have been introduced into our country nearly one hundred and thirty thousand; before 1776, a few more than three hundred thousand."*

The Duke de Rochefoucault Liancourt, who travelled in the United States in 1795, says, "Nearly twenty vessels from the harbors of the United States are employed in the importation of negroes to Georgia and to the West India Isles." The duke designates the merchants of Rhode Island as the conductors of what he calls the "accursed traffic," which they "are determined to persevere in till the year 1808," the period fixed by the Constitution when it is permitted to abolish it; but, he observes, they ship only one negro for every ton of the burden of their vessels, which, moreover, he adds, "are small ones."†

The tables given in the Lords of Council's Report show that a considerable portion of the slavers in those days were but of a hundred tons burden. This was probably the capacity of the Rhode Island slavers. If so, the number of slaves annually carried by each was one hundred only; making, in all, an annual importation by them of two thousand slaves. But a portion of

---

* Bancroft's United States, vol. iii. p. 407.

† Travels by the Duke de Rochefoucault Liancourt, vol. ii. p. 292 (of English translation).

these went to the West Indies,—another proof, it may be remarked, that the demand at home was not great. On the other hand, slaves may have been imported in English bottoms; some were in Dutch; and it is true, as already stated, that a few hundred slaves were annually brought from the West Indies.

Upon the whole, it seems a high estimate to put the annual importation, for some years after the close of the Revolutionary War, at three thousand. During that war, as commercial intercourse with foreign nations was almost wholly suspended, few or no slaves could have been imported; and the trade was probably resumed but gradually after the war. From 1776 to 1790 there were only six years when the trade could be considered open. If we estimate that two thousand five hundred were imported during each of these six years, we have fifteen thousand as the importation from 1776 to 1790.

Let us suppose Bancroft's "a few more than three hundred thousand" to mean three hundred and ten thousand, and we have the total number of slaves imported into the United States up to the year 1790, as follows :—

Up to the year 1776 310,000
From the year 1776 to the year 1790............... 15,000
                                                        ————
        Total imported up to 1790........... 325,000

At this point we emerge, in a measure, into light. The census commences. We know that the colored population of the United States in 1790 was seven hundred and fifty-seven thousand three hundred and sixty-three, of whom fifty-nine thousand four hundred and sixty-six were free. The three hundred and twenty-five thousand that had been imported were in that year represented by seven hundred and fifty-seven thousand three hundred and sixty-three. The colored population of the United States had already considerably more than doubled itself by natural increase.

At the end of the next decade—that is to say, in the year 1800—this population was one million one thousand four hundred and thirty-six; having increased in ten years at the rate of about thirty-two and a quarter per cent.

How much of this accession was due to natural increase, and how much to slave-trade importation?

The rate of increase among the colored population of the United States has been, by the census, as follows :—

In the decade from 1790 to 1800 .... 32.23 per cent.
    do.   1800 to 1810 .... 37.58 "
              [Slave-trade ceases.]
In the decade from 1810 to 1820 .... 28.58 "
    do.   1820 to 1830 .... 31.44 "
    do.   1830 to 1840 .... 23.41 "
    do.   1840 to 1850 .... 26.62 "
    do.   1850 to 1860 .... 21.90 "

During the first decade in which there was no disturbing element by importation of slaves,—to wit, from 1810 to 1820,—the rate of increase was 28.58; during the next decade, 31.44. Let us assume the former as the rate of *natural* increase from 1790 to 1800. Deducting it from the *actual* increase during that period,—namely, 32.23,—we have a remainder of three and two-thirds per cent. as the increase from Africa: that would give twenty-seven thousand seven hundred and seventy as the number of slaves imported in the ten years from 1790 to 1800; or at the rate of two thousand seven hundred and seventy-seven a year.

In the next decade, eight years of which only were open to slave-importation, that importation appears to have greatly increased. The colored population amounted, by the census of 1810, to one million three hundred and seventy-seven thousand eight hundred and ten; exhibiting an increase, in the decade, at the rate of 37.58 per cent. If, as before, we rate the natural increase at 28.58, we shall have nine per cent. on one million one thousand four hundred and thirty-six (that is to say, ninety thousand one hundred and twenty-three) of accession to the population in question, due to other causes than natural increase. But, during this decade,—to wit, in 1803,—Louisiana, purchased from France, became a part of the Union; and her colored population, free and slave, added forty-two thousand two hundred and forty-five to the census-returns of 1810. Deduct this amount from ninety thousand one hundred and twenty-three, and we have forty-seven thousand eight hundred and eighty-four as the number of slaves that may have been directly imported into the United States in the eight years from 1800 to 1808; being at the rate of five thousand nine hundred and eighty-five a year. The rate of importation was evidently increasing with rapidity. Fortunate was it for our country and for the cause of humanity that Congress availed itself of the constitutional provision which permitted, in 1808, the abolition of the slave-trade.

Another item remains to be determined ere we can complete our estimate of importation. Of the colored population which Louisiana brought into the Union, what proportion may we properly ascribe to the slave-trade, and what proportion to natural increase? The total number at the date of purchase appears to have been about thirty thousand.* To supply this number,

---

* By an accurate census of Louisiana, taken in 1785, the total population was twenty-eight thousand five hundred and thirty-seven; of whom

how many had probably been imported under colonial rule?

Except as to difference of nationality in her owners, Louisiana, previous to 1803, was not differently situated from the Southern States of the Union. Part of the same continent, coterminous in her chief boundaries, with similar climate and general condition, there seems no good reason to suppose that the natural increase of her colored population had been at a rate much lower than ours.

But, in 1800, our colored population had very nearly

---

about fourteen thousand were slaves, and one thousand free colored. From that date there seems to have been no separate authentic census of the colony until one was made in 1803 by the Consul of the United States at New Orleans, under orders from the Department of State. From the best documents he could obtain, he put the total population at forty-nine thousand four hundred and seventy-three, but without separating whites and blacks. See History of Louisiana from the Earliest Period, by François-Xavier Martin, New Orleans, 1827, vol. ii. pp. 77, 78, and p.

Other authorities put it higher,—as Major Amos Stoddard, in his "Sketches, Historical and Descriptive, of Louisiana," p. 226. He admits that there are no precise data to determine the population in 1803, but estimates fifty thousand seven hundred whites, and forty-two thousand six hundred colored,—together, upwards of ninety-three thousand. This, however, is clearly an over-estimate; as our own official census of 1810 makes the entire population of Louisiana in that year but seventy-six thousand five hundred and fifty-six. At first sight, the consul's estimate of forty-nine thousand four hundred and seventy-three seems too low; since, if it be not, fifty per cent. was added to the population in the seven years from 1803 to 1810. This would seem improbable, but for the remarkable fact that the entire population of Louisiana (chiefly, of course, by immigration from other States of the Union and from Europe) doubled in the next decade; amounting, in 1820, to one hundred and fifty-two thousand nine hundred and twenty-three.

As a medium term between these conflicting authorities, we may assume the entire population in 1803 to be sixty thousand, of whom half were colored. This agrees with Mr. Carey's estimate. Speaking of the colored population, Mr. Carey says, "Nearly thirty thousand were found in Louisiana at her incorporation into the Union."—*The Slave-Trade, Domestic and Foreign*, p. 17.

trebled its original numbers. Let us suppose (to avoid
the chance of over-estimate) that in 1803 the slaves
and free colored people of Louisiana had only doubled
in number as compared to their African descendants.
That would give fifteen thousand as the number imported into that colony up to the time when it became
part of the United States.*

Summing up these various items, we have the total
number of slaves imported into the United States up to
the date of the abolition of the slave-trade, as follows:—

Up to 1790, as before...	325,000
From 1790 to 1800...	27,770
From 1800 to 1810...	47,884
Imported into Louisiana, previous to her purchase from France...	15,000
Total slaves imported into the United States................	415,654†

* I ought here, in strictness, to add that proportion of the slave
and free colored population of Texas at the time of her admission which
may be supposed to have been due to the African slave-trade. But, in the
first place, it was small,—a very large proportion of the total (it was about
fifty-eight thousand five hundred in 1850, five years after annexation)
being undoubtedly due to natural increase; secondly, we cannot tell how
many slaves may have been taken thither from the United States; and,
lastly, it is more than offset by the fugitive colored population of Canada
and the colonized population of Liberia, neither of which enter into the
United States Census, though both go to increase the total to which the
half-million slaves shipped in Africa for the United States had actually
swelled in 1860.

† An industrious and pains-taking author, accustomed to statistics, makes
the total one-fifth less than this. Mr. H. C. Carey, in his "Slavery, Domestic and Foreign," Philadelphia, 1853, p. 18, after furnishing his reasons
for each separate estimate, sums up as follows:—

Prior to 1714...	30,000
From 1715 to 1750.....................................	90,000
From 1751 to 1760.....................................	35,000
From 1761 to 1770.....................................	74,500
From 1771 to 1790.....................................	34,000
Subsequent to 1790....................................	70,000
Total number imported up to 1808............	333,500

It is to be observed that this is an estimate, not of the slaves that were exported from Africa, destined to the United States, but of those that were actually landed there. If the loss on the voyage was, as we have estimated, twenty per cent.,* the above four hundred and fifteen thousand six hundred and fifty-four negroes represent about five hundred and twenty thousand shipped on the African coast, whether directly for this country or coming by way of the West Indies,—since five hundred and twenty thousand less twenty per cent. is four hundred and sixteen thousand.

If the statement of the Duke de Rochefoucault † that the Rhode Island slavers carried but one negro for each ton burden may be relied on, the average mortality on board slave-ships bound to North America was likely to have been less than twenty per cent. It would, probably, be safe to estimate that out of half a million negroes shipped from Africa, the number above estimated to have reached us may have been landed.

Referring, now, to our estimate of the number of slaves taken from the African coast during the three centuries and a half of the slave-trade,—namely, fifteen millions five hundred and twenty thousand,—we may assert, in round numbers, that *half a million of these went to our own country*, chiefly during its colonial existence, and *fifteen millions to the West Indies and to South and Central America.*

We have now the means of answering the following questions :—What became of each of these two so unequal divisions of this expatriated people? What has

---

I think Mr. Carey has estimated the rate of natural increase in early days, say from 1714 to 1770, too high,—not allowing for the effect, then sensibly felt, of that disproportion between the sexes, incident to the slave-trade, to which we shall hereafter have occasion to advert.

* See page 59, *ante.*   † See page 87, *ante.*

been the respective destiny of each? How are they now represented? The answer involves results so extraordinary, at first sight so incredible,—and, in effect, even when thoroughly examined, so difficult of satisfactory explanation,—that I have devoted much time and labor to the critical revision of the materials whence my conclusions are drawn, before venturing to place them on record.

This is the answer. THE HALF-MILLION SHIPPED FOR NORTH AMERICA HAVE INCREASED NEARLY NINEFOLD,—being represented in 1860 by a population exceeding four millions four hundred thousand; while THE FIFTEEN MILLIONS SENT TO THE WEST INDIAN COLONIES AND TO SOUTHERN AMERICA HAVE DIMINISHED, FROM AGE TO AGE, until they are represented now by LESS THAN HALF THEIR ORIGINAL NUMBER!*

How marvellous, beyond all human preconception, are these results! Had the fifteen millions whose lot was cast in the southern portion of our hemisphere increased in the same proportion as the half-million who

---

* Those who may be tempted to object to this latter calculation, as based in part on approximating estimates, would do well to bear in mind that it is fully borne out by another calculation, already given (pages 63, 64, *ante*), and which is based upon official tables alone,—a calculation covering a period of seventy-four years in the last century, and extending to the entire negro population of the largest English West Indian colony, Jamaica, throughout these seventy-four years: the results, in condensed view, being as follows:—

Negroes in Jamaica in 1702..		41,596
Negroes imported from 1702 to 1775.................	497,736	
Deduct exported from 1702 to 1775.................	137,014	
Leaving in the island imported slaves........................		360,722
Total in 1775, if population had been stationary...	....	402,318
But the actual population in 1775 was........................		192,787

Showing a reduction, in three-quarters of a century, in the negro population of Jamaica, of more than one-half.

were carried to its northern continent, their descendants, instead of dwindling to half, would have been to-day a multitude numbering more than a hundred and thirty millions of men!

CHAPTER IX.

TOUCHING THE CAUSES OF CERTAIN MARVELLOUS RESULTS.

What is the explanation of this startling marvel? Is it to be found solely in the greater humanity with which the negroes of the United States have been treated, as compared with those of other slave countries?

A little research will show us that there were other causes in operation to produce these strange results,—causes chiefly due to the fact that the slave-trade to the United States was brief in its duration and unimportant in its operations, compared to the slave-trade to the West Indies and South America.

But wherever the operations of the slave-trade are of great magnitude, the effect is to check the natural increase of the slave population on plantations.

In the first place, it introduces an unnatural element into that population, which it is proper here to set forth. And to this element a portion of the decrease in the negro population of the countries to which these estimates extend is indisputably to be ascribed.

The abnormality referred to is the uniform practice of dealers, in selecting cargoes of negroes on the African coast, to purchase a considerably larger proportion of males than females. All the witnesses agree in the fact, though they differ as to the motive. Some testify that it was more difficult to procure salable women than men; ascribing this to various causes,—as, to the prevalence of polygamy in Africa, to the fact that there were fewer female criminals than male criminals, also that as to the chief offence for which criminals were sold to slavery, namely, adultery, "it was sometimes pardoned in the women, but never in the men."*

Other witnesses, however, affirm that there was no difficulty in procuring as many female slaves as males. Mr. Eldrid, captain of a slaver from Rhode Island, testifies, "Female slaves can be procured on the coast with more facility than male slaves."† The true motive is probably given by a slave-surgeon, Mr. Falconbridge, who deposes, "On the coast of Africa the captains of slave-ships never wish to purchase more than one-third females. The planters in the West Indies, in many cases, prefer males, because they lose the labor of a female in the latter end of pregnancy and for a little time afterwards."‡

Most of the witnesses state the usual proportion between the two to be three males for one female. The Rev. Mr. Newton says, ".The number of male slaves purchased usually exceeded that of the females in the proportion of four to three, and sometimes of two to three."§

The exact average proportion appears to have been between these two rates. In the Report of the Jamaica House of Assembly, already quoted from,‖ in which this

---

* Testimony of Mr. Miles, Lords' Report, Part I. Sheet O. Mr. Weaver (same page) says, "Few women are sold for any other crime than adultery, and that is very often forgiven them."

† Lords' Report, Part I. Sheet N, 6.

‡ Ibid. Mr. Falconbridge made five voyages as surgeon.

§ Ibid.

‖ Page 57, *ante.*

disparity in the numbers of the sexes is adduced as a chief cause of the decrease in their slave population, tables are given showing the exact proportion in the case of forty-nine thousand one hundred and thirty-five negroes imported by the chief negro-factors into Kingston from 1764 to 1788. Of these, thirty thousand six hundred and thirty-six were male and eighteen thousand five hundred and thirty-nine were female; the relative proportion being, as nearly as may be, five males to three females.

Of each one thousand negroes imported, then, there were, on the average, six hundred and twenty-five men and three hundred and seventy-five women. Each thousand, therefore, was only equal, so far as power of reproduction was concerned, to a population of three hundred and seventy-five men and three hundred and seventy-five women; in other words, to a normally constituted population of *seven hundred and fifty.*

It follows that as to any given West Indian or other slave population, kept up by constant supplies through the slave-trade, we must deduct twenty-five per cent., or, in other words, take three-fourths only of its nominal amount, on which to estimate its power of natural increase.*

To this extent, then, the decrease of population in the West Indies and South America is not to be wholly ascribed to the more cruel treatment or more oppress-

---

* The Committee of the Jamaica House of Assembly from whose Report the above is extracted, fall into a remarkable error. They deduct from the whole number imported *two-fifths,* "to bring the sexes to an equality;" that would be *forty* per cent.,—reducing each thousand to six hundred. But, as each thousand contained three hundred and seventy-five women, it was evidently equal in power of reproduction to a population of three hundred and seventy-five men and three hundred and seventy-five women; in other words, to an ordinary population of seven hundred and fifty.

ive labor to which the slaves were subjected by the planters, but to the policy pursued by the African slave-traders in selecting their human cargoes.

That such a disturbance of a great natural law must have produced immoral results, in an aggravated form, cannot be doubted. As little doubtful is it that this immorality was carried to an excess which still further diminished the rate of natural increase.

As, however, it must be supposed that the slave-traders brought to the market precisely the assortment of cargo which they found the most salable, the above abuse is chargeable indirectly to the planters themselves. Had they desired on their plantations an equal number of each sex, the slave-dealer would doubtless have found means to supply it.*

The slave-trade had another, still more sinister, influence. It is beyond a doubt that wherever that trade prevailed it tended directly to aggravate the condition and to shorten the lives of the plantation slaves. This happened because it increased the temptation to cruelty and overwork. An author who resided twenty years in Brazil, and who has dealt tenderly with slavery, confesses:—

"Until 1850, when the slave-trade was effectually put down, it was considered cheaper on the country plantations to use up a slave in five or seven years and

---

* "Many of the largest and best sugar-estates on the island of Cuba belong to the different ecclesiastical orders. Under the mask of discouraging a vicious intercourse of the sexes, some of them religiously resolved to purchase only male negroes,—a devout austerity which would appear to have originated in the idea that men can do more work than women. Deprived of connections resulting from one of the chief laws of nature, and driven to desperation, the unhappy negroes, not unlike the first Romans, have been known to fly to the neighboring estates, seize on the women and carry them off to the mountains."—*History of the Maroons*, by R. C. Dallas, London, 1803, vol. ii. p. 60.

purchase another, than to take care of him. This I
had in the interior from native Brazilians, and my own
observation has confirmed it. But, since the inhuman
traffic with Africa has ceased, the price of slaves has
been enhanced, and the selfish motive for taking
greater care of them has been increased."*

Of the two influences to check population above
indicated as flowing directly from the slave-trade, the
first, connected with the disparity in the numbers of
the sexes, is totally insufficient to account for the
unexampled decrease in the fifteen millions of slaves
sent to the Gulf and to South America. Suppose that
entire population, when it left the shores of Africa, to
have been in the proportion of five men to three
women : its power of natural increase would have
equalled only that of a normally constituted population of eleven millions two hundred and fifty thousand.
But had the slaves in question actually numbered but
eleven and a quarter millions, and had they increased
in the same proportion as the half-million shipped for
the United States have done, the census-return of
their descendants to-day would have been ninety-eight
millions,—more than three times the population, white
and black, of the United States.

The immoral influence of the disparity in the relative
numbers of the sexes already alluded to, and its tendency to check population, is here to be taken into
account. But that disparity prevailed among imported negroes only, and did not, of course, extend
beyond the first generation. Unquestionable as the
tendency of the influence in question was to diminish
the rate of natural increase, we can receive it only as

---

* Brazil and the Brazilians, by Rev. D. P. Kidder, D.D., and the Rev.
J. C. Fletcher, 1857. It is Mr. Fletcher who writes the above.

a partial element, not seriously affecting the general result.

Thus the marvellous variance in the fate of the two divisions of negro immigrants is not explained, though the exact figures are somewhat varied, by the disproportion of the sexes in these immigrants.

As to the second influence, growing out of the temptation gradually to work to death laborers who can be replaced any day by fresh purchases, it is hard to believe that it should have exerted over human cupidity so terrible a sway as to cause the reduction to seven and a half millions of men of a population which, had they been treated and had they thriven but as well as the slaves of the United States, would have numbered to-day ninety-eight millions of souls.

Climate may have had something to do in working out the ultimate results; yet there is no evidence to show that the climate of the West Indies and of Brazil is less suited, or more fatal, to the negro than that of our Slave States.

A more influential circumstance, especially in the West India islands, was the habitual absenteeism of many of the proprietors The slaves were left at the mercy of overseers, often uncultivated and mercenary, who had no interest in their preservation so long as those who died could be profitably replaced by what were called "new negroes." Most of these overseers were unmarried men; and writers on the condition of the colonies frequently allude to the fact that, when this was the case, the lack of female care and considerate forethought as regarded the slave mothers and children had a very considerable influence in diminishing the population.

Upon the whole, however, it must be confessed that,

while the general facts in this case are indisputable, the explanations we have so far suggested seem inadequate to account for the extraordinary results we have disclosed.

CHAPTER X.

WAS THERE A FAILURE AND A SUCCESS?

But the lesson taught to mankind by this stupendous crime is far beyond the marvel of, its results. Four years ago that lesson was, in part, foreshadowed only, and could not have been fully read. To-day it is written in terrible characters all over the history of our country.

Four years ago it might have been said with a certain plausibility that the experiment of human slavery had two phases,—the phase of failure and the phase of success.

With a certain plausibility only, it is true. There has been success in this country, so far as the mere physical increase of the slave population can attest the fact,—no further. But population has increased in the world in spite of ceaseless wars, in spite of constant vice and misery. It increased in famine-stricken Ireland. It increased in England throughout the term of that feudal system which made of the island one great military camp. It increased in France throughout the centuries of that old régime of which the insufferable iniquities were at last requited by popular vengeance and culminated in the first Revolution.

It is to be admitted, however, that an annual increase, from natural causes alone, of two and three-

quarters to three per cent., prevailing throughout a
term of years in any population (as among the slaves
of the United States from 1810 to 1830), indicates that
they have not been subjected to the extremity of hardship which marks the fate of negro slaves in other portions of this hemisphere.   And as, even to the present
day, the rate of natural increase among slaves in this
country has been considerable. it may be fairly inferred
that slavery in the United States, even in its latter and
severer phase. has been. as a general rule, more merciful and lenient than in the West Indies and South
America.

It will probably be claimed, in addition. that it indicates a very considerable amount of physical comfort
and well-being.   But any such admission would con-
vey a false impression in regard to the actual condition
of the slave, especially in the Cotton and Sugar States.
The investigations of the Government commission, of
which for a year past I have been a member, thoroughly convince me that the statements made in our
Preliminary Report as to the condition of the slave
population of South Carolina apply substantially to
that of Georgia. Alabama, Mississippi, Texas, and
Arkansas, and, with no very considerable modifica-
tions, to Louisiana, to Florida, to a few portions of
North Carolina, and to the western half of Tennessee.

I repeat here, as applicable to the States above
named, that which, antecedent to more general exa-
minations, we had predicated only of South Carolina :—

"This is one of the States in which the system of
negro slavery seems to have reached its furthest de-
velopment, with the least modification from contact
with external civilization.   There it appears to have
run out nearer to its logical consequences than in any

other we have visited. There it has been darkening
in its shades of inhumanity and moral degradation
from year to year, exhibiting, more and more, increased
cruelty, a more marked crushing out, in the case of
the negro race, of the humanizing relations of civilized
life, and a closer approach, in practice, to a monstrous
maxim,—the same which a chief-justice of the Supreme
Court, perverting history, alleges to have been the
sentiment of the civilized world when the United
States Constitution was adopted, and in the spirit of
which he assumes (in virtue of such perversion) that
Constitution to have been framed,—namely, that 'the
negro has no rights which the white man is bound to
respect.'* The evidence before the commission shows
that, half a century ago, its phase was much milder
than on the day when South Carolina seceded. It is
the uniform testimony of all emancipated South Carolinian slaves above the age of sixty, that their youth
was spent under a state of things which, compared to
that of the last thirty years, was merciful and considerate. As a general rule, these old men are more
bright and intelligent than the younger field-hands;
in many of whom a stolid, sullen despondency attests
the stupefying influence of slave-driving under its more
recent phase.

  "The disintegration of the family relation is one of
the most striking and most melancholy indications of
this progress of barbarism. The slave was not permitted to own a family name: instances occurred in
which he was flogged for presuming to use one. He
did not eat with his children or with their mother:
'there was no time for that.' In portions of this State,

---

* Dred Scott vs. John F. A. Sandford, December Term, 1856.—23 Howard,
407.

at least, a family breakfast or dinner table was a thing
so little known among these people, that ever since
their enfranchisement it has been very difficult to
break them of the life-long habit that each should
clutch the dish containing his portion and skulk off
into a corner, there to devour it in solitude. The entire day, until after sunset, was spent in the field; the
night in huts of a single room, where all ages and
both sexes herded promiscuously. Young girls of
fifteen—some of an earlier age—became mothers, not
only without marriage, but often without any pretence of fidelity to which even a slave could give that
name. The Church, it is true, interposed her protest;
but the master, save in exceptional cases, did not sustain it, tacitly sanctioning a state of morality under
which ties of habitual affection could not assume a
form dangerous or inconvenient to despotic rule.

"The men, indeed, frequently asked from their masters the privilege of appropriating to themselves those
of the other sex. Sometimes it was granted; sometimes, when the arrangement was deemed unprofit-
able, it was refused. Some cases there were in which
a slaveholder, prompted by his own sense of morality
or religion, or urged thereto by a pious wife, suffered
these connections of his slaves to have the sanction of
religious ceremony. But it is evident that to connect
even with such a quasi-marriage the idea of sacredness
or religious duty was inconsistent with that legal
policy of the Slave States which forbade to render in-
dissoluble among slaves a relation which to-morrow it
might be for the interest of their owner to break up.

"The maternal relation was often as little respected
as the marital. On many plantations, where the system was most thoroughly carried out, pregnancy neither

exempted from corporal punishment* nor procured a
diminution of the daily task; and it was a matter of
occasional occurrence that the woman was overtaken
by the pains of labor in the field, and the child born
between the cotton-rows. Humane masters, however,
were wont to diminish the task as pregnancy advanced,
and commonly gave three, occasionally four, weeks'
exemption from labor after childbirth. The mother
was usually permitted to suckle her child during three
months only; and the cases were rare in which relaxation from labor was allowed during that brief period.
On the other hand, instances have occurred in which
the more severe drove the negress into the field within
forty-eight hours after she became a mother, there to
toil until the day of the next birth.

"A noble exception, among others, to such a system
of inhumanity, gratefully testified to by the negroes

---

* "Another of my visitors had a still more dismal story to tell. Her
name was Die: she had had sixteen children, fourteen of whom were dead.
She had had four miscarriages: one had been caused from falling down
with a very heavy burden on her head, and one from her arms strained
up to be lashed. I asked her what she meant by having her arms tied
up. She said their hands were first tied together, sometimes by the
wrists, and sometimes—which was worse—by the thumbs, and they were
then drawn up to a tree or post, so as almost to swing them off the
ground, and then their clothes rolled round their waist, and a man with a
cow-hide stands and stripes them. I give you the woman's words. She
did not speak of this as any thing strange, unusual, or especially horrid
and abominable: and when I said, 'Did they do this to you when you were
with child?' she simply replied, 'Yes, missis.' * * * I gave the woman
meat and flannel, which were what she came for, and remained choking
with indignation and grief long after they had all left me to my most
bitter thoughts."—*Journal of a Residence on a Georgian Plantation* in
1838-39, by Frances Anne Kemble, p 200.

Mrs. Kemble says, elsewhere in her Journal, "Never forget, in reading
the details I send you, that the people on this plantation are well off, and
consider themselves well off, in comparison with the slaves on some of the
neighboring estates."

who enjoyed it, was to be found on the plantation of
ex-Governor Aiken, one of the largest and most influential planters in the State.   His habitual clemency,
it is said, gave umbrage to many of his neighbor planters, as endangering their authority under a severer rule.

"Under such a slave system as this, where humanity
is the exception, the iron enters deep into the soul.
Popular songs are the expression of the inner life; and
the negro songs of South Carolina are, with scarcely an
exception, plaintive, despondent, and religious.   When
there mingles a tone of mournful exaltation, it has
reference to the future glories of Zion, not to worldly
hopes.

"If to the above details touching slave-life in this
State we add the fact that, because of the unhealthy
climate of the sea-islands off the South Carolinian coast
(chiefly due, it is said, to causes which may be removed),
the least valuable and intelligent slaves were usually
placed there,—further, that, being much isolated in small
communities, these slaves frequently had children of
whom the father and mother were near blood relatives,
producing deterioration of the race,—it can excite no
surprise that the negroes of South Carolina, as a class,
are inferior to those from more Northern States.   An
intelligent negro from a northern county of North
Carolina, who had there learned the blacksmith's trade,
and had been hired to work on a railroad in South
Carolina, stated to the Commission that he never knew
what slavery really was until he left his native State.
While there, he was comparatively contented.   Within
a month after he reached South Carolina, he determined to risk his life in an attempt to escape."*

---

* Preliminary Report of the American Freedmen's Inquiry Commission,
pp. 3 to 10.   It was prepared by the Author.

To judge whether a natural increase of population is necessarily connected with physical comforts, it behooves us to look to the interior slave-life of the South, to the motives which encourage such increase, and to the conditions which attach to it. We find these well set forth by one who had the best opportunities to observe,—having resided some five months on her husband's plantation in Georgia, and being in the habit of recording, from day to day, events as they occurred. It is doubtful whether there has been presented to the public, in modern times, a more authentic or more faithful chronicle of every-day life in the Cotton States than is to be found in the Journal from which our extract is taken. The writer had been conversing with a negress who had formerly been a favorite house-servant, and thus proceeds :—

"She named to me all her children,—an immense tribe ; and, by-the-by, E——, it has occurred to me that whereas the increase of this ill-fated race is frequently adduced as a proof of their good treatment and well-being, it really and truly is no such thing, and springs from quite other causes than the peace and plenty which a rapidly increasing population is supposed to indicate. * * * Peace and plenty are certainly causes of human increase, and so is recklessness. Here it is more than recklessness; for there are certain indirect premiums held out to obey the early command of replenishing the earth, which do not fail to have their full effect. In the first place, none of the cares—those noble cares, that holy thoughtfulness which lifts the human above the brute parent—are ever incurred here either by father or mother. The relation, indeed, resembles, so far as circumstances can possibly make it so, the short-lived connection between the animal and its young. * * * But it is not only the absence of the conditions which God has affixed to the relation which tends to encourage the reckless increase of the race; they enjoy, by means of numerous children, certain positive advantages. In the first place, every woman who is pregnant, as soon as she chooses to make the fact known to the overseer, is relieved from a certain portion of her work in the field, which lightening of labor continues, of course, as long as she is so burdened. On the birth of a child, certain additions of clothing and an additional weekly ration are bestowed on the family; and these matters, small as they may seem, act as powerful inducements to creatures who have none of the restraining influences actuating them which belong to the parental relation among all other people, whether civilized or savage. Moreover, they have all of them a most distinct and perfect knowledge of their value to their owners as property; and a woman thinks, and not much amiss, that the more frequently she adds to the number of her master's live-stock by bringing new slaves into the world, the more claims she will have upon his consideration and good will. This was perfectly evident to me from the meritorious air with which the women always made haste to inform me of the number of children they had borne, and the frequent occasions on which the older slaves would direct my attention to their children, exclaiming, 'Look, missis! little niggers for you and massa; plenty little niggers for you and little missis.' "*

We have had abundant evidence of the correctness of the view here taken. General Saxton, for example, deposes :—

---

* Journal of a Residence on a Georgian Plantation in 1838-39, by Frances Anne Kemble, New York, 1863, pp. 59, 60.

Question.—"Were the women, under the slave-system, taught chastity as a religious duty?"

Answer.—"No, sir. They were taught that they must have a child once a year."*

The prohibition against suckling their children longer than three months is part of the same system.† The result is that the slave families are usually very numerous. We found in South Carolina, among the freedmen, several instances in which the mother had had twenty children and upwards in as many years. The result is disclosed, beyond possible denial, throughout Mrs. Kemble's graphic volume. Excessive child-bearing, coupled with ceaseless toil,—an interval of three weeks only being allowed after childbirth,—these are conclusively shown to have been the source of shocking diseases and terrible suffering to the female slaves.‡

The argument to be deduced from the great natural increase of the slave population in the United States would be much stronger than it is, had the ratio of increase, as it was during the two first decades after

---

* Preliminary Report, already cited, p. 13.

† Among the witnesses whose testimony is given in the Report of the Lords in Council are several physicians residing in the island of Jamaica. One of these, Adam Anderson, of the parish of St. Ann, testifies, "Great losses are sustained in the increase of negroes from the length of time the negro women continue their children at the breast, seldom less than two years, and many of them more."—*Lord's Report*, Part III., Jamaica, Appendix No. 7.

If this habit was common throughout the colonies, its effect, taken in connection with the custom so widely different in our Slave States, is to be enumerated as one among the most influential causes which went to produce the great variance of results as to increase of slave population in the West Indies and in the United States.

‡ Journal of a Residence in Georgia. See page 29; also 39,—a very bad case: also pages 79, 122, 190, 191, 192, 196, 214, 215, 233, 251, with very strong evidence; and many others. The whole work is a most dreary picture,—a terrible daguerreotype of what daily negro life was, in a Cotton State, before the war.

the abolition of the slave-trade, been kept up to the present day.

But it has not been kept up. I have already had occasion, in the extract cited from the Preliminary Report of our Commission, to advert to the fact that the system of slavery among us has been increasing in severity and hardship from year to year,—especially for thirty years past. A glance at the census shows that statistics confirm what we had deduced from personal observation. From 1830 the rate has been gradually diminishing; for, as the Superintendent of the Census remarks. "The greater apparent increase among slaves from 1840 to 1850 is connected with the admission of Texas in 1845."* In these thirty years the ratio of natural increase has diminished over ten per cent. in the decade, or one per cent. a year.

At the same diminishing ratio, less than quarter of a century would have witnessed a state of things under which the slave population would have been annually decreasing. Whether it would have fallen still lower, until, as in Jamaica and other West Indian islands, the deaths had so far exceeded the births that in less than a century half the population would have disappeared, must now ever remain—let us thank God!—a matter of conjecture.

The duration of slavery, as a system, in the United States, has been but brief, as compared with its prolonged existence in West Indian colonies. Here that system had not borne its deadliest fruits. Here, especially for four or five decades after the Revolutionary War, certain features of a patriarchal† character tended to alleviate its harshness.

---

* Preliminary Report of Eighth Census, p. 7.

† We have found indications of this in taking the evidence of freedmen.

But, in all its various phases, that system which confers on one race the fatal privilege of idleness at expense of forced drudgery imposed upon another race, differs rather in the degree than in the character of its results. These results are, as a general rule, wherever slavery exists at all, essentially and degradingly evil,—evil to the victim of the injustice, evil as certainly to the inflicter of it; for there is no human crime that does not recoil on the criminal.

Alike in the Slave States of the Union as in the colonies of the West Indies and in every other land in which the system of slavery prevails, its victims may be said to live deprived, directly or indirectly, of every natural right.

One of the most universal objects of human desire and of human endeavor is the acquisition of property. But the laws of Slave States forbid that the slave shall ever acquire any. The holiest of human relations is marriage. But a slave cannot legally contract it. The dearest of human ties are those of family. But a slave may see them broken forever, without redress, any hour of his life. Of all human privileges the highest is the right of culture, of moral and mental improvement, of education. But to the slave the school is forbidden ground, reading and writing are penal offences. The most prized of personal rights is the right of self-

---

especially in the more northern Slave States. Mrs. Wilkinson, a colored woman in Canada West, testified, "I was raised in Winchester, Virginia. * * * I have seen a good deal of hard treatment of others, but never had any myself. I was brought up like one of the family. I used to call my master 'father' and the old lady 'mother,' until I came to this country. That is the way I was raised." This woman was set free by her mistress after her master's death.—*Supplementary Report A, on the Refugees from Slavery in Canada West,* by one of our Commission, Dr. Samuel G. Howe, p. 98.

defence. But a slave has it not; he may not resist or resent a blow, even if it endanger limb or life.

What remains to the enslaved race? Life to man? Honor to woman? Any security for either? Nominally, yes; actually, save in exceptional cases, no. In the statute laws against murder or rape, the word *white* is not to be found. Persons of either color *appear* to be equally protected. But among the same statutes, in every Slave State of the Union, is incorporated a provision to the following or similar effect :—

" A negro, mulatto, Indian, or person of mixed blood, descended from negro or Indian ancestors, to the third generation inclusive, though one ancestor of each generation may have been a white person, whether bond or free, is incapable of being a witness in any case, civil or criminal, except for or against each other."*

As far as regards the two worst crimes against the person, the above provision is the exact equivalent of the following :—

" Murder or rape by a white person, committed against a negro, mulatto, Indian, or person of mixed blood, descended from negro or Indian ancestors, to the third generation inclusive, though one ancestor of each generation may have been a white person, shall go unpunished, unless a white person shall have been present and shall testify to the commission of the crime."

The apology for a law according to which a woman cannot testify against the violator of her person or a son against the murderer of his father, is. that in a community where negro slavery prevails. such a provision is necessary for the safety of the white race. The

---

* Code of Tennessee, 1858, § 3808. p. 687. I have selected this section from the code of one of the Middle States, as a fair, average example.

same apology is adduced to justify the taking from the slave the right of property, of marriage, of family ties, of education, of self-defence.

The apology may be valid. It may not be possible to force one race to hopeless labor, they and their children after them, from sunrise till sunset, day after day, year after year, till death,—thus to toil unrequited save by the coarsest food and clothing,—in order that another race may exist in idleness; it may not be possible safely to carry on such a system without depriving the laboring race of every right, civil and social, and of every protection to life and property, for which man has been struggling through all the centuries of history.

It may be one of the conditions of safety to the master race, thus usurping the labor of their fellows, that some of their own children should be as utterly disfranchised as the imported African. The phraseology of the section we have quoted is very suggestive: "to the third generation inclusive, though one ancestor of each generation be white," are the words. The white man makes the law, and his son, his grandson, his great-grandson, so that these share, to the extent of one-eighth, the blood of the attainted race, may, whether slave or free, be murdered with impunity if the murder be not committed in the presence of some one without that eighth of taint. The white man makes the law, and exposes the chastity of his own daughter—fairer of skin, it may be, than himself—to brutal outrage, without possibility of bringing the ruffian who commits that outrage to justice, unless the wretch, adding folly to infamy, selects his opportunity when one of his own race happens to be within hearing or sight.

These may all be necessary conditions, without

which, under the slave-system, domestic tranquillity cannot be maintained.

Let us assume that in this matter the slaveholder is in the right, and that while slavery exists these are his conditions of safety. What then? In what sense, except a blasphemous one, can we pronounce that system to be successful which cannot maintain itself except in violation of every principle of justice and virtue which God has implanted in the heart of man,—except by the abrogation as to an entire race of men of those rights of property, of family, and of person, to assert and maintain which, in all ages of the world, good and brave men have willingly sacrificed life?

But there are other conditions, not set forth in statute law, with which the existence of slavery is inseparably connected,—those, namely, which affect the masters of slaves.

Of all forms of prayer none is more strictly adapted to the nature and the wants of man than this:—"Lead us not into temptation." Men in the mass cannot be habitually tempted with impunity. It was said of One only that He was tempted like as we are, yet without sin.

But of all human temptations one of the strongest and most dangerous is that which attends the possession throughout life of arbitrary and irresponsible power. As a rule, it is always abused. A beneficent despotism is the rarest of exceptions. This is one of the great lessons of history, upon which is based the doctrine of popular rights and the theory of a republican government.

Under no phase of society has the operation of the law which connects sin with ceaseless temptation been more apparent than in states where slavery prevails. One of our greatest statesmen, himself a sufferer under the evils he deprecates, has set forth in strong terms the practical results.

"There must, doubtless," said Jefferson, "be an unhappy influence on the manners of our people, produced by the existence of slavery among us. The whole commerce between master and slave is a perpetual exercise of the most boisterous passions,—the most unremitting despotism on one part, and degrading submissions on the other. Our children see this, and learn to imitate it, for man is an imitative animal. * * * The parent storms, the child looks on, catches the lineaments of wrath, puts on the same airs in the circle of smaller slaves, and, thus nursed, educated, and daily exercised in tyranny, cannot but be stamped with its odious peculiarities. The man must be a prodigy who can retain his manners and his morals under such circumstances."*

It has been customary to illustrate the influence of slavery on the dominant race by adducing individual examples of barbarous cruelty exercised towards slaves by their masters.† These might be multiplied inde-

---

* Jefferson's Notes on Virginia, chapter on Customs and Manners, p. 270.

† A single example from among many that came to our notice may here suffice. It is selected as exhibiting the uncontrolled passion and fearful inhumanity of that spirit, bred by arbitrary and irresponsible power, which could visit with terrible punishment a light and venal offence. It was testified to by an eye-witness, a respectable colored mechanic, Solomon Bradley by name, who was employed for several years on the railroad between Charleston and Savannah.

One morning this witness, going for a drink of water to a house near the line of the railroad, occupied by a Mr. Farraby, heard dreadful screams in the door-yard. Looking through an aperture in the board fence, he saw a woman stretched, face downward, on the ground, her hands and feet bound to stakes. Over her stood her master, striking her with a leathern trace belonging to his carriage-harness. As the strokes fell, the flesh of her back and legs was raised in welts and ridges. Occasionally, when the poor creature cried out with insufferable pain, her tormentor

finitely; but they are less conclusive of the effects inseparable from the system than the picture drawn by Jefferson, the exact truth of which every one familiar with the interior of Southern society will admit.

Slavery breeds imperiousness of manner, impatience of contradiction or delay, ungovernable passion, contempt of labor. While it produces a certain carelessness of wealth and easy profuseness in expenditure, it discourages hardy enterprise in useful fields. Habits of regulated industry are seldom formed within the sphere of its influence,—its tendency being to substitute for

---

kicked her in the mouth, to silence her. When he had exhausted himself by flogging, he called for sealing-wax and a lighted candle, and, melting the wax, dropped it on the woman's lacerated back. Then, taking a riding-whip and standing over the poor wretch, he deliberately picked off, by switching, the hardened wax.

While this scene of torture was acted, Mr. Farraby's grown-up daughters were looking on, from a window that opened on the yard.

Afterwards, Bradley made inquiry of the woman's fellow-servants as to what crime she had committed, and was told that it consisted in burning the edges of the waffles she had been cooking for breakfast!

"The sight of this thing," the witness added, "made me wild, and I could not work right that day. I prayed the Lord to help my people out of their bondage."

This witness was born and brought up in a northern county of North Carolina, where, he said, such cruelty was unheard of. Slaves were flogged there; but if one broke away during the punishment, no attempt was made to renew it.

What a fearful addition to the atrocities of this scene, that the young women were witnesses of the ungovernable rage and savage cruelty of a father! And what must have been the character of the father who could thus expose himself before his children? The least evil that could result was that it excited within them detestation of their parent. More probably the influence was brutalizing,—deadening in their young hearts the sentiment of humanity, and preparing them to become themselves, in after-life, merciless tyrants on the slightest provocation.

Outrages so gross may not have been common even in South Carolina; but, when they did occur, they passed unnoticed either by law or by public opinion. What must have been the state of that society in which crimes so grave were committed with utter impunity?

these indolent fashions of dependence and of luxurious self-indulgence. It weakens the supremacy of law, with its sobering and chastening influence. It engenders, in young men especially, a spirit of reckless daring, a sort of careless courage that takes little account of human life, a love of violent excitement, sometimes running into military ardor, and ever liable to take the form of gambling, or intemperance, or that debasing licentiousness which must needs prevail wherever, in any class or race, female chastity is neither respected by custom nor protected by law.

Hence a state of society in which, with manners often cultivated, with an impulsive generosity and free hospitality to equals in station, there mingles a certain essential barbarism, which not only shows itself habitually in the treatment of those occupying servile or inferior positions, but also breaks out, towards others, in bursts of temper so frequent and violent that the old regulator in ages when force was law,—the wager of battle,—in its modern form of duel, is openly sanctioned by public opinion, as a necessary check to social insult or lawless outrage.

These remarks apply in their full force to society as it existed, at the time the Southern insurrection declared itself, in the States we have designated as those in which the slave-system has been fully developed,—the States which first rebelled,—the States which will be the last to return to their allegiance. No reflecting and dispassionate observer who has sojourned in any of these States long enough to become familiar with their manners and morals and social condition will pronounce the view I have taken of the results of slavery to be intemperate or unfair. From one or other of these results no man or woman born and bred in a slave community, no matter whether they learn to approve slavery or to hate it, can be reasonably expected wholly to escape.

It is true as to the Border States, where the tilled estates more frequently assume the aspect of farms than of plantations, where the owner and his sons sometimes work along with the slaves, and, even where they do not actually work with them, yet personally superintend their labor so as to recognize and take interest in them as individual human beings, it is true, and should here be stated, as to these States, that the phase of slavery there existing is sensibly modified, and is divested, more by practice, however, than by relaxation of law, of some of its most odious features. On small estates especially, slaves in the Border States often have, by sufferance, a certain amount of property, continue to live, by sufferance, as if legally married, are frequently trusted with important charges, are sent to market with cattle or produce, are consulted in regard to the management of the estate. Under such circumstances they are greatly improved by coming into daily contact with white persons; and instances occur in which they are treated by the family with as much consideration as if their skin exhibited no tinge of African blood.

In these States the chief aggravation of the system is the inter-State slave-trade, the forcible separation of families to fill up those melancholy gangs, assorted like droves of cattle, and whose destination is to that mysterious and undefined land, the terror of the border negro, known to him only as "down South."*

* This domestic slave-trade appears to have been increasing rather than diminishing up to the commencement of the war. Judge Ballard, of Louisville, deposed, before our Commission, "A few years since, more cruelty, I think, was tolerated by the sentiment of the State than when I was a boy. We saw, more frequently, negro gangs driven through the city. Formerly

But even under this comparatively moderated phase of slavery, the inherent injustice of the system exhibits itself in the character of the very indulgences which in other Slave States are forbidden by law.* In visiting the colored population of Louisville, this presented itself in a marked manner to the notice of our Commission.

I found living there many slaves who, as the usual phrase is, had "hired their time." One case was of a slave woman, apparently fifty years of age, named Charlotte. She had been hiring herself for more than fifteen years. She had two children, one thirteen, the other seventeen, both of whom worked in a tobacco-factory. Their regular wages were two dollars a week each; sometimes they did extra work, earning more. She hired their time also. For herself and these two children she paid her owner *five dollars* a week,—a dollar a week for herself, and two dollars a week for each of the children. She had brought up these children without any aid whatever from her master, feeding

---

a man did not like to be seen in that position; but five or six years ago it became quite common. There was no effort to conceal the thing. I recollect well that thirty years ago I knew a man who was a physician in this city, to be tried by his church for the offence (committed as administrator of an estate) of unnecessarily separating, by sale, a slave from his wife." *Testimony taken by the Commission in Kentucky*, pp. 38, 39.

* "No person shall hire to any slave his time; nor shall any person owning the legal or equitable title of any slave, absolutely or for a term of time, his agent or attorney, or other person having the control of a slave, wilfully permit or suffer such slave,—

"1. To own hogs, cows, horses, mules, or other like property.

"2. To trade in spirituous liquors, hogs, cows, horses, or mules, or provisions, or other like property.

"3. Nor, as if he were a free person of color, to live by himself.

"4. To hire himself out.

"5. To work and labor.—to spend his or her time, or to do other acts." *Code of Tennessee*, 1858, § 2685, p. 578.

them, clothing them; and this she continued to do even now, when her master took their wages. She inhabited with them a single room in a tenement house, about twelve feet square, paying her own rent. She supported herself by washing. A large bed and an ironing-table, which together filled up most of the room, were piled with clothes prepared for ironing when I entered.

This woman made no complaint, and did not appear to regard her condition as one of unusual hardship. The only thing she seemed to have expected from her master was a little aid in sickness. In reply to a question as to what he did for her, she answered, "My master never gives me any thing, not even a little medicine, no more than if I did not belong to him." As her appearance indicated feeble health, I made inquiry on that score, to which she replied that she "was ailing," but that she "managed to keep up enough to make her wages." She added, "I get along well enough and keep the hire paid up; you could not pay me to live at home if I could help myself." I asked her if she had to pay the hire for her boys in any event; and her reply was, "If the boys make more than two dollars a week apiece, I get what is over; if they don't make that, I have to make it good to him; he has got to have it Saturday night, sure."

Another case was marked by an additional feature. It was that of a slave woman, apparently about thirty-five years of age. Coming upon her without any notice of our visit, I found her in a room tidily kept and herself decently dressed. She had been hiring herself for eleven years, at seventy-two dollars a year. Her husband, she told me (of course he could not be legally such), was a slave, and was hired by his master as cook in one of the Louisville hotels for three hundred dollars a year; out of this his master, she said, gave him, once or twice a year, a five-dollar note,—nothing else. There were in the room two bright, intelligent-looking children, one a boy about ten years old, the other a girl two or three years younger. One might go, at a venture, into a dozen dwellings of persons of the middle class in fair circumstances, and not find their children cleaner in person or more neatly and suitably clad than were these two young slaves. I expressed to the mother my satisfaction at their appearance. Her face saddened, and she said, "The white people have two of my children, and that boy is about big enough to go."

I inquired how this was, and she informed me that her master left her children with her till they were about eleven years old, and then took them home to work. Up to that age she fed and clothed them at her own expense. The last they had taken was a little girl between eleven and twelve years old. Four months ago the mother had gone to the plantation to visit her, not having seen her then for ten months; she had saved a dress for the child, and took it with her. "I knew," she said, "that she would need it, but I never expected to find her as bad as she was; I could not help crying when I saw her; she was not dressed as a human creature should be; I took off her rags and washed her. She was serving my young master, and he had whipped the child so that you could not lay your hand anywhere along her back where he had not cut the blood out of her. I did all I could for her, and dressed her, but I could not stay. [Here the poor creature's eyes filled with tears.] I brought back the rags my child was covered with; I have them yet." I asked to see them. She went out, it seemed reluctantly, and brought a small bundle of filthy tatters, which she appeared ashamed that I should see. "If I could only have kept the children," she said, "I would not have cared for all the rest. I liked so much to have them clean and nice."

This woman made her living, as I ascertained, solely by washing and ironing. She, like the other, had paid her expenses of every kind, the doctor's bill inclusive.

Truly the tender mercies of slavery are cruel! Under what other system would men, assuming to be gentlemen, commit towards poor, hard-working women such flagrant injustice as this?

In the first case, the woman Charlotte, in feeble health, advancing in years, with no means of living except labor in washing and ironing, pays to her master two hundred and sixty dollars a year for the privilege of supporting by such labor herself and her children. The man who received this human rental had literally furnished no equivalent. For more than fifteen years the woman had not received from him even a little aid in sickness. The children for whom he now demanded a yearly payment of a hundred dollars each had cost him nothing. For fifteen years the mother had fed and clothed them, cared for them in sickness and in health; she continued, unrequited, to feed and clothe them still. Who, if not that mother, was entitled to their wages now? Who, except one in whom slavery had blunted every perception alike of justice and delicacy, would consent to receive and to use money coming from such a source as that?

In the second case, three hundred and seventy-two dollars annually had been paid for eleven years by the woman and him whom she called her husband, the law of the State forbidding that she should be his lawful wife. Four thousand and ninety-two dollars the master had received from them in that time; for which he had rendered nothing except some ten dollars a year in the form of a gratuity to the man. Was this four thousand dollars considered by the master enough to take from these two working-people? The mother, in this case as in the former one, had brought up her children at her own expense, had fed them and had clothed and kept them as any respectable yeoman might have been glad to see his children clothed and kept. Were the father and mother, after the payment of this four thousand dollars, after the care and cost of bringing up these children, suffered to enjoy the comfort of having them with them, and the aid which, as they grew up, they might be able to afford? No. While the children were a burden, that burden was thrown on the mother,—she, too, as in the other case, earning a living as washerwoman. As soon as they were of an age to be of service, they were removed to the plantation. And how treated there? The young girl was taken, neatly and comfortably clad, from her mother's care. One would have thought that the most common regard for decency, to say nothing of justice, would have suggested that the worse-than-orphaned child should have been kept, as the servant of a rich man, at least as reputably as the poor slave-mother had kept her. Yet she was suffered to go about the house, before her master's eyes, in filthy rags. One would have supposed that the recollection of the four thousand dollars received from the hard-working parents might have risen up to save—if Christian feeling could not save—this poor child, deprived of natural protectors, from brutal cruelty. Yet she was treated as no man with the least pretence to humanity would have treated a dumb beast.

Let no one say that these were cases of unusual hardship. The parties themselves evidently did not con-

sider them such. There was no tone of querulous
complaint. The facts came out only in answer to my
direct inquiries; and neither of the women seemed to
consider herself especially to be pitied. Charlotte
thought a little hard of it that her master did not send
her medicine when she was sick. The hire of her children did not seem to have suggested itself to her as any
injustice. Even the other said she would be willing to
part with the children if she only knew they were well
treated. Had she been suffered to retain them, her
gratitude to her master for his generosity would, it was
evident, have been unbounded. One could see that the
four thousand dollars subtracted from her own and her
husband's earnings never occurred to her except as a
usual thing.

Both women expressed the greatest satisfaction that
they were allowed to hire themselves. It was sufficiently apparent that nothing short of compulsion
would cause either of them to return to what they still
called "home." What sort of home could that be, compared to which the privilege of hard labor at the wash-
tub, purchased by a weekly payment in money,—coupled
in one case with a similar payment for the children and
in the other with the loss of them,—was regarded as a
favor and a blessing?

Let us not imagine that the masters, in these two
cases, were sinners above all men that dwelt in Kentucky. They may have been indulgent in their own
families, kind to their white neighbors, honorable in
their business dealings, esteemed in society. The anom-
aly is presented of men whose characters in one phase
entitle them to be called cultivated and civilized, yet
in another—to wit, in their dealings with a proscribed
race—exhibiting such utter disregard of the mild graces
of Christianity—mercy, charity, long-suffering, kindness,

and good will to men—that it is not too harsh to say they live in a state of semi-barbarism. Such results are chargeable far less to the individuals who have thus gone astray than to the system which has formed their character. But a system has lamentably failed that results in the arrest of human civilization and Christian progress, in injury to the national character, and in disregard, under any circumstances, of the natural and inalienable rights of man.

Nor is the contempt engendered by this system towards those occupying subordinate social positions confined to the colored man. Under slavery there grows up a class of white, as well as black, Pariahs. A marked feature in Southern society is the temper and demeanor of the wealthy slaveholder towards an indigent portion of his own race,—the "poor whites," as they are called, of the South. Slavery is to them the source of unmingled evil. Labor owned, competing with labor hired, deprives them of the opportunity to earn an honest livelihood. Labor degraded before their eyes destroys within them all respect for industry, extinguishes all desire by honorable exertion to improve their condition. Doomed by habitual indolence to abject poverty, complacently ignorant, vilely proud, it is doubtful whether there exists, in all civilized society, a class of men more deplorably situated. And yet how fiercely have they been brought to fight for the slave-masters who despise them, and for the system which consigns them to degradation!*

---

* While visiting Nashville as commissioner, I encountered a notable specimen of the class I have been describing.

It was in the office of a gentleman charged with the duty of issuing transportation and rations to indigent persons,—black and white. There entered a rough, dirty, uncouth specimen of humanity,—tall, stout, and wiry-looking, rude and abrupt in speech and bearing, and clothed in

Such a system is fraught with mischief politically as well as morally. They who violate the rights of one race of men lose a portion of their reverence for the rights of all. It comes to this, that the peculiarities of character stamped, more or less, on every country in which slavery exists, are, in spirit and in practice, adverse not to religion and civilization alone, but to democracy also. No people exposed to the influences which produce such peculiarities will ever be found imbued with a universal sense of justice, with a respect for industry, with a disposition to grant to labor its just position among mankind. Nor can any people subjected to influences so deleterious ever be expected to remain, in perpetuity, contented and happy under republican rule.*

---

threadbare homespun. In no civil tone, he demanded rations. While the agent went to consult the Governor, I discovered from the man's boastful manner that he was a rebel deserter, who had " seen as much of fighting as he wanted." When he was informed that all the rations applicable to such a purpose were exhausted, he broke forth :—" What am I to do, then?   How am I to get home ?"

" You can have no difficulty," replied the agent.   " It is but fifteen or eighteen hours down the river [the Cumberland] by steamboat to where you live; I furnished you transportation; you can work your way."

" Work my way !" (with a scowl of angry contempt.)   " I never did a stroke of work since I was born, and I never expect to, till my dying day."

The agent replied, quietly, " They will give you all you want to eat on board, if you only help them to wood."

" Carry wood !" he retorted, with an oath.   " Whenever they ask *me* to carry wood, I'll tell them they may set me on shore. I'd rather starve for a week than to work for an hour. I don't want to live in a world that I can't make a living out of without work."

The insolent swagger with which this was said ought to have been seen to be fully appreciated.   All over the man—in his tone, manner, language, and degraded aspect—was stamped his class; the most ignorant, illiterate, and vulgar.   He seemed fitted for no decent employment upon earth except manual labor; and *all* labor he spurned as a degradation.

* " After dinner the conversation again turned on the resources and power of the South, and on the determination of the people never to go

In no sense, then, neither political, moral, or religious, can the experiment of slavery in these States be regarded in any other light than as an utter failure.

CHAPTER XI.

THE GREAT LESSON.

ALL this might have been said four years ago, in reply to any argument that might then have been adduced in support of the assertion that slavery, though it failed in the West Indies and South America, had succeeded in the United States.

But how instructive, how invaluable, the experience of these eventful four years! New views of the subject present themselves to-day. Aspects of the slavery question, hidden until now, come conspicuously into the light. History had previously recorded the social and economical evils of the system. Now she has presented to us its political consequences.

And now, therefore, going back to our starting-point on the African coast, and following up, once more, the two diverging branches of the great stream of slave-immigration, flowing West,—the one branch bearing half a million captives to this Northern continent, the

---

back into the Union. Then cropped out again the expression of regret for the rebellion of 1776, and the desire that, if it came to the worst, England would receive back her erring children, or give them a prince under whom they could secure a monarchical form of government. There is no doubt about the earnestness with which these things are said."—*My Diary, North and South*, by William Howard Russell, 1862, chapter xvii.

This was in April, 1861, on a South Carolinian plantation. "The *rebellion* of 1776;" outspoken enough, certainly. Mr. Russell represents these sentiments as then common in the South.

other conveying fifteen millions to islands and a continent farther South,—we are able, by the light of recent experience, to present, more fully and clearly than ever before, the comparative results in either case.

Increase or decrease, apparent success or undeniable failure, the ultimate results have been fatal alike.

The fifteen millions despatched to the West Indian colonies and to South America never, as a population, took healthy root in the lands to which they were banished. They had no growth. From the first, and ever after, century by century, they melted away under the influences of the system that degraded and destroyed them. Their fate, and the lesson it conveyed, were immediate and apparent. God stamped the policy which enslaved them, at every stage of its progress, with his reprobation.

But as to the half-million that came among us, the mark of Divine condemnation, apparently suspended for a time, came in a different form at last. For a time that half-million increased and multiplied and replenished the earth. For a time their masters were wealthy and prosperous, as men usually rate prosperity. For a time these masters increased in political power. They held sway in the Republic. They controlled the National Legislature; they obtained a majority of the public offices. The end was delayed. And when it came at last, it was the direct result of the peculiarities of character impressed by slavery on its votaries. Imperious and insubordinate, they rebelled against lawful authority. Spurning wholesome control, they rejected the President who was the choice of the majority. Despising a working people, they sought to sever connection with the North, a race of unblushing laborers. Seduced by evil habit into the belief that man's noblest condition is to live by the exertions of others, they

undertook to erect a separate political system, of which
slavery was to be the corner-stone.

Thus did slavery bring on a civil war between
brethren of the same race and tongue and faith,—a
war wide-spread and embittered and desolating as
wars have seldom been. Thus will slavery have caused
the violent death, in the country which tolerated it, of
half a million of free people. Thus will slavery leave
behind it, in the country where it held its millions in
bonds, a public debt little short, it may be, of that
which loads down the industry of Great Britain.

If God, in his mercy, shall in the end preserve us
from results to which these deaths and losses are but
as dust in the balance; if our punishment does not
extend to dismemberment, anarchy, extinction as a
great nation; if lookers-on from European courts are
not to moralize on the ignominious failure of the noblest
experiment to reconcile democratic liberty and public
order that was ever instituted by man; let us remember
how narrowly we shall have escaped; let us call to
mind what days of gloom we have passed through,
how often, as the contest proceeded, victory has hung
even-balanced in the scale, and what a little thing,
amid the thousand contingencies which our short sight
calls chance, might have turned the issue against us
forever!

In our case, the Great Lesson was long delayed. But
how terrible in its actual results, how awfully impressive
in its possible consequences, when it came upon us at
last!

The conclusion of the whole matter is this. Review-
ing, from its inception on this continent down to the
present hour, the history of that offence against humanity by which one race, in order to escape labor,
usurps by violence and appropriates to itself the labor

of another, we find that the tendency of that usurpation is always to debase the usurpers, and, usually, to extinguish the laboring race, and that in the only notable exception to this last rule the effects of this sin against justice and mercy culminated in the bloodiest civil war that ever arose among men,—of the horrors and sufferings incident to which we cannot even now see the end.

If a calm review of this terrible episode in modern history bring no conviction that the crime which we are now expiating in blood must be atoned for, as crime can only be, by practical repentance,—by thrusting out from among us the Wrong of the Age,—argument will be unavailing. If, as all signs of the times appear to indicate, the nation has already attained to this conviction, then it behooves us to consider how we shall carry it into effect,—whether and in what manner we can effect emancipation by legal and constitutional means.

The consideration of these questions shall form the subject of the following chapters.

PART II.

EMANCIPATION.

"To deliver an oppressed people is a noble fruit of victory."—
VATTEL: Book III. § 201.

PART II.

EMANCIPATION.

CHAPTER I.

A MIXED QUESTION OF CONSTITUTIONAL AND INTERNATIONAL LAW.

I PROPOSE to inquire whether the act or acts whereby the slaves heretofore held in insurrectionary States were declared free are, or are not, absolutely legal and irrevocable.

Seldom, throughout all history, has there been presented to any nation, for its decision, a question of greater import than this. Its solution involves not alone the social destiny of three or four millions of human beings, but also the permanent peace and the national honor of one of the great Powers of the world. It allies itself also, in an especial manner, to the progress of civilization.

The events of the last three years have radically changed the legal aspect of this subject. Questions once purely constitutional have now become complicated with questions of international law.

A member of the commonwealth of Christendom, our republic is bound by the acknowledged rules of that unwritten code, governing the society of civilized nations, of which the foundation and the sufficient authority is the common consent and usage of that society.* We are as much bound by its rules as we are by the provisions of our Federal Constitution. In proportion as civilization advanced, "it became," says Sir James Macintosh, "almost as essential that Europe should have a precise and comprehensive code of the law of nations as that each country should have a system of municipal law."†

Engaged in war, we must conform to the Law of Nations, so far as that law regulates public rights and duties during war. We must take from it, for example, the extent of our rights as regards enemies' property, and the limitations of these rights.

In interpreting the International Code, however, it behooves us to bear in mind that, as its office is to foster civilization in peace and to mitigate suffering and repress outrage in war, the sentiment of Christendom, taking practical form, has been gradually moulding its rules from the more to the less severe. Thus, among the Romans, the rule that renders enemies' property liable to confiscation was so harshly enforced that it was made to apply to subjects of the enemy who, at the breaking out of war, happened, innocently and by the accident of travel or temporary commerce, to be residing among them. But Grotius and Vattel argue that, as these foreigners entered the country under the sanction of public faith, the government which permitted this tacitly contracted that they should be protected while there and allowed a reasonable time to return, taking with them their movable effects. And

---

* We search in vain for any other authority for the Law of Nations than is to be found in Grotius' favorite phrase, "*Placuit gentibus.*"—*De Jure Belli et Pacis,* l. ii. cxviii. 4, s. 5.

† Lecture on the Law of Nature and Nations, by Sir James Macintosh.

this practice, from its evident justice, has now super-seded the stricter enforcement of the rule.

Beyond all doubt, as a nation holding itself second to no other in its desire to aid the cause of humanity and civilization, our practice in war ought to conform to the milder and more enlightened phase of sentiment sanctioned by modern publicists. But in so doing it behooves us to see to it that the scruples of moderation do not degenerate into weakness, defeating their own object, and protracting the term of a war which is a disgrace to the age if it be not regarded as God's agency for a great purpose. We are guilty of culpable negligence if we fail to employ all the means which are legally and properly within our reach, to bring to a close, at the earliest practicable day, the struggle which now desolates and depopulates our land. There is no just war which has not for its object (on a rightful basis, it is true) the speedy restoration of peace.*

In pursuing that object, as the legal phrase is, *viâ facti*, in other words, by the compulsory means of war, injury must be inflicted on the enemy. States, being in the nature of vast corporations, are not, indeed, liable to punishment; but acts resembling punishment, though in fact but measures of self-defence, become necessary, if we resort to war at all. "It is to be remembered," says an able modern commentator on International Law, "that, as the will of the subject is bound up in that of his government, it may well be that the consequences of the conduct of his rulers may be attended with injury both to the person and property of the subject, and that the enemy is justified in striking through them at the government from which

---

* "Bellum pacis causa suscipitur."—*Grotii Proleg.* 25, *de Jure Belli et Pacis,* lib. i. c. i. s. i.

he has received a wrong for which redress has been denied."*

The just limit, in this case, is set forth by Montesquieu. "Nations," says he, "owe to each other, in peace, the greatest amount of good, and in war the least amount of evil, that is compatible with their true interests."†

Guided by these general considerations, I proceed to examine the question of Emancipation, legally considered.

In so doing, it may simplify the matter if I offer a few preliminary observations.

CHAPTER II.

CONSTITUTIONAL ASPECT OF WHAT IS CALLED SLAVE PROPERTY.

THERE has been radical diversity of views on this subject. Extreme opinions, on either side, have been confidently urged,—one party alleging that the Federal Constitution admitted and sanctioned property in human beings, another, that its very preamble utterly excluded that idea, and that none of its provisions recognized, or could recognize, in any sense, rights of property that are contrary alike to law and to morality.

We cannot reach clear ideas of the constitutionality of Emancipation, under any circumstances, until we

---

* Commentaries on International Law, by Robert Phillimore, M. P., vol. iii. p. 69.

† "Le droit des gens est naturellement fondé sur ce principe, que les diverses nations doivent dans la paix le plus de bien, et dans la guerre le moins de mal, qu'il est possible, sans nuire à leurs véritables intérêts."— MONTESQUIEU: *De l'Esprit des Lois*, l. i. c. iii.

settle, in advance, under what phase and to what extent the social relation known as slavery is recognized (if it be recognized) by the Constitution of the United States. And throughout the prosecution of such an inquiry it behooves us to bear in mind the great fundamental ideas of human liberty and natural rights to give legal force to which that instrument was originally framed. It behooves us, further, to keep in view a well-established legal principle, founded on justice and identified with civilization, laid down by the Supreme Court of the United States in these words:—"Where rights are infringed, where fundamental principles are overthrown, where the general system of the law is departed from, a legislative intention must be expressed with irresistible clearness, to induce a court of justice to suppose a design to effect such objects."*

The constitutional provision regarding the slave-trade, cautious in its phraseology, was temporary only, ceasing to operate after the year 1808, and need not, therefore, be considered.

There are but two other provisions that bear on this subject, familiar to all; for they have been the theme of a hundred excited discussions,—one, contained in the fourth article and second section of the Constitution, being in these words:—

"No person held to service or labor in one State, under the laws thereof, escaping into another, shall, in consequence of any law or regulation therein, be discharged from such service or labor, but shall be delivered up on claim of the party to whom such service or labor may be due."

The claims to service or labor here referred to may

---

* United States against Fisher, 2 Cranch, 390.

be for years or for life: both are included in the above
provision. In point of fact, there were existing, at the
time that provision was adopted (as there still exist),
both classes,—the first class, for a term of years, then
consisting, in part, of claims against foreign adults who
had bound themselves to service for a limited time to
repay the expenses of their emigration, but chiefly, as
now, of claims to the service or labor of what were
called apprentices, usually white minors; the second,
for life, were claims to the service or labor of men,
women, and children of all ages, exclusively of African
descent, who were called slaves.

The first class of claims were found chiefly in Northern
States, the second chiefly in Southern. There was a
great disparity between the numbers of the two classes.
While the claims to service or labor for years numbered
but a few thousands, there were then held to service or
labor for life five or six hundred thousand persons; and
the number has since increased to about four millions.

The constitutional provision is, that persons from
whom, under the laws of any one State, service or labor
is due shall not be exonerated from the performance of
the same by the laws of any other State to which they
may escape. The apprentice, or the slave, shall in that
case, on demand of the proper claimant, be delivered
up.

Such a provision involves the recognition of certain
rights of property; but of what kind?

Is the ownership of one human being by another
here involved? Is the apprentice, or the slave, recognized in this clause as an article of merchandise?

State laws regulating apprenticeship and slavery may
give to the master of the apprentice, or of the slave,
the custody of the person and the right of corporal
punishment, in order the better to insure the perform-

ance of the labor due. These laws may declare that an apprentice, or a slave, who strikes his master, shall suffer death. They may provide that the testimony of an apprentice, or of a slave, shall not be received in any court of justice as evidence against his master. They may make the claims to service or labor, whether for years or for life, transferable by ordinary sale. They may declare such claims to be, under certain circumstances, of the nature of real estate. They may enact that these claims shall be hereditary, both as regards the claimant and the person held to service; so that heirs shall inherit them, and also so that the children of apprentices, or of slaves, shall, in virtue of their birth, be apprentices or slaves. They may deny to the slave, or to the apprentice, during the term of slavery or of apprenticeship, legal marriage, education, the ownership of property real and personal. But State laws and State Constitutions, whatever their varying provisions, cannot modify or affect, expressly or by implication, the Constitution of the United States. They have no power, direct or indirect, over it. It controls them. The Supreme Court has decided that "the Government of the Union, though limited in its power, is supreme within its sphere of action;" and again, paraphrasing the Constitution itself, that "the laws of the United States, when made in pursuance of the Constitution, form the supreme law of the land, any thing in the Constitution or laws of any State to the contrary notwithstanding."*

Therefore no State action can add to, or take from, the Constitution of the United States. Therefore State laws and State Constitutions, valid within their own

---

* McCulloch against the State of Maryland, 4 Wheaton, Rep. p. 316. Constitution of the United States, section 6.

municipal jurisdiction, are without force within the proper sphere of Federal authority. They can neither determine the interpretation of the Federal Constitution, nor serve as commentary or explanation of its intent. It is an authority superior to theirs; and it is to be interpreted by the words, fairly and candidly construed, of its framers.

These words deny to any State the right either to pass laws or regulations discharging from service or labor inhabitants of another State, held to such service, who may have escaped therefrom, or to refuse, to the proper claimant of such service, the surrender of the fugitive by whom it is due. They do this. They do nothing more. And this denial of the right, on the part of any State of the Union, to defeat certain claims to labor held by citizens of another, is a protection afforded to *all* claims for labor alike,—to that of the master seeking a white apprentice, and to that of the master seeking a negro slave.

There is an evident intention, so far as words can mark intention, to go no further. There is an evident intention to refrain from any expression that might be construed into an acknowledgment of slavery as a social institution. Nothing could be more notorious than the fact of its existence as such in many of the States then about to be united in one Federal Union. But the responsibility of that existence is studiously left to the States who permit it. It is adverted to as a fact, not sanctioned. If, while it exists, it is protected in one of the incidents which belong alike to it and to apprenticeship, the reason is to be found in the necessity of the case. It is evidently with no other intent than to avert angry conflicts between State and State, that an individual State is not permitted to release from involuntary labor any person who, by the municipal rule of another State, is subjected to such labor.

This view of the case is fully borne out by the remarkable phraseology of the provision under consideration. The word *slave*, though then universally used to designate a negro held to service or labor for life, is not employed. We know, from the debates in the Convention which framed the Constitution, that this peculiarity was not accidental; nor can we overlook the inevitable inference thence to be deduced. This provision does not recognize slavery except as it recognizes apprenticeship. African slavery, according to the expressly selected words, and therefore according to the manifest intent, of the framers of the Constitution, is here recognized as a claim to the service or labor of a negro,—nothing more, nothing else.

It avails not to allege, even if it were true, that in 1787, when these words were written, a negro was commonly considered property. Chief-Justice Taney, delivering the decision of the Supreme Court in the Dred Scott case, asserts that in the thirteen colonies which formed the Constitution, " a negro of the African race was regarded as an article of property." If the opinion expressed on this subject, by a large majority of those who sat in deliberation in the various States, on the adoption of the Federal Constitution, as recorded by Eliot, is to be received, as it properly may be, in evidence to prove the probable opinions of their constituents on this subject, then has the chief-justice's assertion no foundation in truth.* But, true or not, it has no legitimate bearing on the argument. Let the

---

* Any one who will examine, as I did, a carefully-prepared abstract of the opinions on slavery, favorable and unfavorable, expressed in the various State Conventions during the debates on the adoption of the Federal Constitution, may satisfy himself that this statement is correct.

facts as to popular opinions in Revolutionary days be as they may, they are but the opinions of individual colonists; and these cannot be received as a basis of construction for the words, nor can they rebut the plain intent, of a constitutional provision. It is not what individual colonists believed, but what the framers of the Constitution incorporated in that instrument, that we have to deal with.

They avoided the use of the word "slave." They incorporated the words "person held to service or labor." They admitted the existence, under State laws, of the claim to service or labor, none other,—a claim (regarded in its constitutional aspect) in the nature of what the law calls a *chose in action*, or, in other words, a species of debt,—a thing to which, though it cannot be strictly said to be in actual possession, one has a right.

In common parlance we employ words, in connection with slavery, which imply much more than such a claim. We say slaveholder and slave-owner; we speak of the institution of slavery; but we do not say apprentice-holder or apprentice-owner, nor do we speak of the institution of apprenticeship. The reason, whether valid or invalid, for such variance of phraseology in speaking of the two classes of claims, is not to be found in any admission, express or implied, in the provision of the Constitution now under consideration. The framers of that instrument employed one and the same phrase to designate the master of the apprentice and the master of the slave. Both are termed "the party to whom service or labor may be due."

The employment of the popular phraseology referred to, indicating social disabilities and a subjection of one race to another, which originated in local legislation alone, has had a tendency to mislead public opinion as to the actual connection between slavery and the

Federal Constitution. The mass of our people had come to think, at last, not only that the claim to labor was recognized, and was protected in cases where the denial of that claim might have led to a dangerous conflict of authority between States,—which was true,—but also that the framers of the Federal Constitution, straying off from the landmarks set up by the Declaration of Independence, had recognized as just, and had pledged the nation to defend against all comers, a social institution under which one human being became the chattel of another,—which was false.

If we were to regard the Constitution as endorsing slavery in all its changing phases, shaped by successive State laws and institutions as these phases have been, whither might not the doctrine have led us? Among the ancient Romans the master had the power of life and death over his slave. Let us suppose that South Carolina had enacted, as she might have enacted, a statute granting to her slaveholders this terrible power. Is the Federal Constitution, because of such statute, to be understood as recognizing the doctrine that murder is no crime if perpetrated on the person of a negro held to labor? Instinctively we reject an inference so monstrous that we must have lost all respect for the best men of the Revolutionary period before we could adopt it.

The second and only other provision of the Constitution which refers to slaves (Article 1, Section 2) remains to be considered, in these words:—

" Representatives and direct taxes shall be apportioned among the several States which may be included within this Union according to their respective numbers, which shall be determined by adding to the whole number of free persons, including those bound to service for a term of years, and excluding Indians not taxed, three-fifths of all other persons."

To avoid mistakes, it was deemed necessary to include apprentices by express specification. Why this? Every one would have felt it to be absurd, if the words had been "the whole number of free persons, including farm-laborers." But why absurd? Because persons engaged in free labor are, beyond question, free persons. Not so those "bound to service." While so bound, apprentices may be considered not free; when the "term of years," and with it the bondage to service, expires, they become free, or, as the common phrase is, "their own masters." It was necessary and proper, therefore, to specify whether, in the enumeration of inhabitants, they were to be estimated as free persons or as persons not free.

But would there be any fairness in construing this clause into an admission, by inference or otherwise, that an apprentice, while "bound to service," is a slave? Clearly not. He is a person not free for the time, because another has a legal claim to his service or labor. The Constitution admits this,—nothing more.

And so of slaves. "Other persons" they are called, in contradistinction to "free persons,"—therefore, persons not free; and properly so called, seeing that, like the apprentice before his term expires, they are "bound to service," and that, unlike him, they remain thus bound for life.

But unless we admit that the apprentice, bound to service for a season, is a slave during that season, we cannot justly allege that, by this provision of the Constitution, the negro, held to service or labor for life, is recognized as a slave.

A mere technical view of a great political question is usually a contracted one, of little practical value, and unbecoming a statesman. "The letter killeth, but the spirit giveth life." Yet we must not mistake for technicality a careful interpretation, distinctly warranted by the terms employed, of a public instrument. Every public instrument, by which the governed delegate powers to those who govern, should be strictly construed.

We know very well that the men who framed the Constitution regarded a negro held to service or labor, not, indeed (to speak of the majority of opinions), as a chattel, but as a slave. It would be absurd to argue that temporary claims to the number (let us suppose) of thirty or forty thousand may compare in importance with life-long claims to the number of four millions. The first are of comparatively trifling moment, have never moulded or greatly influenced society among us, and might drop out of our social system without serious disturbance. The latter constitute a system that has roots deep-struck in the social structure of half our country; that involves vast industrial interests; that has gradually obtained influence so great and assumed proportions so gigantic as to become a political element, overshadowing and controlling. It cannot properly be dealt with except after the gravest deliberation and the most sedulous examination, in advance, of every step we propose to take. It cannot be eradicated without producing disturbances such as convulse a nation.

But it is none the less true that neither the number of slaves nor the magnitude of the interests involved can properly influence the judgment in determining the just construction of a clause in the Constitution, or properly set aside a fair deduction from the wording of that clause as to its true spirit and intent. It is none the less true that the framers of the Constitution, in studiously avoiding the employment of the word "slave," undeniably abstained from admitting into that instrument any thing which the use of that word might have implied. Therefore the Constitution does not recognize the ownership of one human being in another. In it we seek in vain any foundation for the doctrine declared by Chief-Justice Taney, that persons held to service or labor for life are articles of property or merchandise.

In one restricted sense, and only in one, is slavery recognized by the Constitution of the United States; as a system under which one man, according to State laws, may have a legal claim to the labor of another.

It follows that the question whether the Federal Government has the right, under any circumstances, to emancipate slaves is more simply and more distinctly stated when put in these words: Has the Federal Government the right, under any circumstances, to take and cancel claims to the service or labor of persons of African descent, held, under State laws, in certain portions of the United States?

If there are circumstances and conditions under which such claims can be legally taken and disposed of by the Government, then, under these circumstances and conditions, Emancipation is constitutional. If there are none such, it is unconstitutional.

This opens up the next branch of our inquiry. And, as we are at war with one portion of the Slave States and at peace with another portion, the question subdivides itself accordingly. For the rules as to property of an enemy during war differ entirely from those which regard the property of peaceful citizens.

Let us, then, first examine the question in its connection with the insurrectionary States.

CHAPTER III.

THE CONSTITUTIONALITY OF EMANCIPATION IN THE INSURRECTIONARY STATES.

HAS the Federal Government the right to take and cancel claims to service or labor held by inhabitants of the insurrectionary States?

An antecedent question is: Are these inhabitants, without distinction as to individual loyalty or disloyalty, and because of their residence within a given territory, enemies of the United States?

Vattel has treated, as fully and as humanely as any other writer on international law, of the rules of that law so far as they apply to civil war. He says:—

"When, in a republic, the nation is divided into two opposite factions and both sides take up arms, this is called a civil war. * * * A civil war breaks the bands of society and government, or, at least, suspends their force and effect. It produces in the nation two distinct parties, who consider each other as enemies. * * * These parties stand in precisely the same predicament as two nations who engage in a contest and have recourse to arms."*

In accordance with these views, the Supreme Court has decided that, because of the present insurrection, there exists civil war. The opinion of the court, delivered in March of last year, is as follows:—

"When the regular course of justice is interrupted by revolt, rebellion, or insurrection, so that the courts of justice cannot be kept open, civil war exists, and hostilities may be prosecuted on the same footing as if

---

* The Law of Nations, by Vattel, Book III. §§ 292, 293.

those opposing the Government were foreign enemies invading the land."*

When one nation is engaged in war against another, all the inhabitants of the latter, without regard to their opinions as to the justice of the war on the part of their own Government, become enemies of the former. If Great Britain, siding with the South, were to declare war against us, John Bright, though he might retain the same friendly sentiments which he now entertains towards this country, would be, in law, the enemy of the United States.

Vattel sets forth this principle in plain and explicit terms :—

"When the sovereign or ruler of the State declares war against another sovereign, it is understood that the whole nation declares war against another nation. Hence these two nations are enemies, and all the subjects of the one are enemies to all the subjects of the other."†

Strictly in accordance with the above, the Supreme Court has given its opinion in the case already referred to. After reciting that the territory "held in hostility to the United States" has a "defined boundary,"‡ which can be crossed only by force, the court adds :—

---

* Claimants of Schooners Brilliant, &c. vs. United States, March Term, 1863. Opinion by Grier, J.—*Amer. Law Register*, April, 1863, p. 338.

† Vattel. Book III. § 70.

‡ This boundary, earlier defined by the respective acts of secession, was officially declared by proclamation of the President, issued under date of July 1, 1862. This was done in accordance with a requisition contained in the second section of an act of Congress, approved June 7, 1862. The list includes eleven States, reckoning Eastern Virginia as one. It does not include Western Virginia, nor Maryland, nor Delaware, nor Kentucky, nor Missouri. Nothing here said, therefore, applies to the constitutional rights of the inhabitants of any of these States. To a proper understanding of the legal points involved, it is indispensable to bear in mind which States are, in the eye of the law, insurrectionary, and which are not.

"All persons residing within this territory, whose property may be used to increase the revenues of the hostile power, are, in this contest, liable to be treated as enemies. * * * Whether property be liable to capture as enemies' property does not, in any manner, depend upon the personal allegiance of the owner."*

According to this decision, property of every kind held by residents of the insurrectionary States, no matter what their personal sentiments or political proclivities may be, is enemies' property. It becomes such in virtue of the domicil of the owner, and of the fact that it "may be used to increase the revenues of the hostile power."

It follows that so much of the law of nations as relates to the right of a belligerent to take or destroy the property of an enemy applies in this case to the property of every inhabitant of the insurrectionary States, without regard to his individual loyalty or disloyalty.

What are the rules of international law which bear upon this matter?

Grotius lays down the principle on the broadest ground. He says:—

"Moreover, by the law of nations, not only he who carries on war for just cause, but also any one engaged in regular war, may, without limit or measure, take and appropriate what belongs to the enemy; so that both he, and all who claim under him, are to be defended in possession thereof."†

---

* Case cited, Claimants of Schooners Brilliant, &c., Amer. Law Register for April, 1863, pp. 343, 344.

† "Ceterum jure gentium non tantum is qui ex justâ causâ bellum gerit, sed et quivis in bello solenni et sine fine modoque dominus fit eorum quæ hosti eripit, eo sensu nimirum ut a gentibus omnibus et ipse et qui ab eo titulum habent in possessione rerum talium tuendi sint."—GROTIUS, l. iii. c. vi. s. 2.

Vattel is quite as explicit. He says :—

"We have a right to deprive our enemy of his possessions, of every thing which may augment his strength and enable him to make war. This every one endeavors to accomplish in the manner most suitable to him. Whenever we have an opportunity, we seize on the enemy's property, and convert it to our own use; and thus, besides diminishing the enemy's power, we augment our own, and obtain at least a partial indemnification or equivalent, either for what constitutes the subject of the war, or for the expenses and losses incurred in its prosecution."*

The Supreme Court, in the case already cited, endorses this well-known principle of international law :—

"The right of one belligerent not only to coerce the other by direct force, but also to cripple his resources by the seizure or destruction of his property, is a necessary result of a state of war."†

These authorities settle the question as to the legality of one enemy taking or destroying the personal property of another.

In a general way, however, a belligerent does not become the legal owner of any personal property belonging to his enemy so long as it is still in that enemy's hands. To obtain a right to it, he must reduce it to possession. "Owner of all property taken from the enemy," says Grotius. "We seize on the enemy's property and convert it to our own use," says Vattel. The Supreme Court employs a similar phrase, authorizing "the seizure or destruction of enemies' property." Until we seize the horses on which the enemy has mounted his cavalry, or the muskets which he has placed in the

* Vattel. Book III. § 161.
† Case cited, Amer. Law Register for April, 1863, p. 341.

hands of his soldiers, they are not ours. As to tangible property, such as horses and muskets, we must capture before we own.

When we propose to take and cancel enemies' claims to service,—in other words, to emancipate the slaves of our enemies,—does the rule hold good ? Must we obtain possession of the persons of these slaves before we can declare them to be free of their bondage ?

In this case, the question is not of seizing and destroying tangible property belonging to the enemy. Even if a slave were an article of merchandise, we do not propose to ourselves the possession and the destruction of that article. If we did, it could not be ours to possess until we captured it, nor to destroy until the laws against murder were repealed.

The property with which we propose to deal, and of which we seek to deprive our enemies, is property of a character very different to that of property in horses or muskets. It consists of a right, or claim,—the only right over a slave by a master which is recognized in the Constitution,—the claim to that slave's service or labor.

This is, strictly speaking, a species of property in the nature of a demand, to be satisfied in the future. It is a debt, of a peculiar nature, it is true,—not payable in money, not recoverable by suit in court, enforced by physical means,—but still essentially a debt. Service or labor is due. It is, indeed, an involuntary debt, not growing out of contract between debtor and creditor, but yet as binding as State laws can make it,—as practically binding, within the State which enacted these laws, as the debt an artisan might contract if he gave, in payment of property brought, his promissory note for so many months' labor. It is a debt due by an inhabitant of the United States to an enemy of the United States.*

Property of this description, being of an intangible character, cannot be physically seized or destroyed. It is evident, therefore, that the usual rule that the seizure, by physical force, of enemies' property must precede our ownership of the same, can have no practical application in this case.

But debts can be confiscated; and, after being confiscated, they can be cancelled so that the debtor shall be forever free of the same. Nor is there in the international code any rule or law to the effect that, before such confiscation or cancelling, the person of the debtor shall be seized, or that the debt cannot be confiscated or cancelled while the debtor is in the enemy's country. If there be legal authority to confiscate, that suffices.

Is there legal authority in this case? Has the Government of the United States, at war with the holders of these claims, the right to confiscate them?

Vattel, in defining what is to be considered as enemies' property liable to confiscation, says:—

---

* The question is not mooted here whether, because of the existing civil war, slaves held within the insurrectionary States are, in law, enemies or not. We have seen that the principle on which the inhabitants of the insurrectionary States, without reference to personal loyalty, are held to be enemies, is, first, because of their domicil, and secondly, because their property may be used to increase the revenue of the hostile power. But slaves are persons acting under duress; they have no voluntary domicil, and cannot legally hold any property, real or personal.

In any event, though by international law the government may rightfully hold all the inhabitants of the insurrectionary States as enemies, it is not compelled to hold them as such. It may undoubtedly waive its right as to the whole or any part of them.

The question is a new one, that has never, probably, been decided by the courts. Its decision is immaterial to the present argument. A debt due to an enemy by any inhabitant of the United States, whether friend or enemy, may lawfully be confiscated. That is good law, and that suffices in the present case.

"Among the things belonging to the enemy are likewise incorporeal things,—all his rights, claims, and debts."*

The expression is of the most comprehensive character; "all his rights, claims, and debts;" embracing beyond possible question, the claims or debts we have now under consideration. We shall search in vain for any special recognition of the right to confiscate that peculiar species of claim,—seeing that neither common law nor international law recognizes the existence of human slavery, or provides rules for its treatment during war. We can be governed, therefore, only by the general rule as to confiscation of claims or debts. But that is explicit and all-sufficient.

Chief-Justice Marshall, in delivering the opinion of the Supreme Court in the case of "Amity Brown versus The United States," said:—

"The right of the sovereign to confiscate debts being precisely the same with the right to confiscate other property found within the country, the operation of a declaration of war on debts and on other property found within this country must be the same."†

Justice Story, though dissenting from the opinion of the court in this case, concurs in the above principle. These are his words:—

"I take upon me to say, that no jurist of reputation can be found who has denied the right of confiscation of enemies' debts."‡

There are no exceptions to this rule which apply to the case we are considering. It is true that, by the modern and milder interpretation of the law of nations,

---

* Vattel, Book III. § 77.
† Amity Brown vs. The United States, 3 Curtis, p. 48.
‡ Case cited, 3 Curtis, p. 61.

there are certain relaxations as to the power of confiscating the rights, claims, or debts of an enemy; for example, in the case of rights granted by a third party to whom it is not a matter of indifference in whose hands they are vested.* Nor is it any longer the law, though it used to be, that sums of money due by neutral nations to our enemy can be confiscated as other property.† Nor are the debts of alien enemies, contracted in the country during peace, to be deemed confiscate solely in virtue of a declaration of war.‡ But none of these exceptions, nor any others recognized by the law of nations, have reference to the present case, in which the question regards debts due to the enemy by inhabitants of our own country. Such debts are, beyond all controversy, liable to confiscation.

It is to be conceded that the precise case, as it here presents itself, may be regarded as *sui generis*. A parallel case cannot, probably, be found in all history,—a case in which, during a civil war, a question touching the confiscation and cancelling of certain claims or debts due by one portion of the inhabitants of an insurrectionary district to another portion of the same rises to the grandeur of a great measure involving not only the peace, but the national existence, of the Power which proposes to confiscate. This could only occur when, as in the present instance, these claims constitute the basis of a vast labor-system endangering domestic tranquillity and imperilling the national unity and life.

A case so unique might well be regarded as demanding the establishment of a precedent. The courts might

---

* Vattel, Book III. ? 77.
† 1 Chitty's Commercial Law, p. 423. 1 Chitty's Law of Nations, pp. 82 to 86.
‡ Amity Brown *vs.* United States, 3 Curtis, p. 46.

well be called upon to decide it on the broad principle that whatever is essential to the preservation of the national life, the Government may lawfully do; just as an individual may, without imputation of murder, take the life of an assailant, when such killing is necessary to save his own life. But it is satisfactory to reach the conclusion that the right to adopt this great measure of national self-defence can be justified even on technical grounds, as involving a confiscation never before exercised. perhaps, by a belligerent, on so grand a scale, but in strict conformity to the law of nations in the premises.

It is, therefore, in every view of the subject, lawful to seize or confiscate and cancel that large class of enemies' debts known, in the language of the Constitution. as " claims to service and labor." It is lawful, by the proper authority, to confiscate these not only when the debtor is within our own lines, but in whatever portion of our country he may happen to be.

What is the proper authority in this case? By whom can these claims be legally cancelled?

Evidently, by the same authority which may legally seize and appropriate any other property of the enemy. Primarily. then, by the sovereign or law-making power of the government, and secondly, when the exigencies of war demand it, by the duly-constituted military authority.

But the chief military authority of the United States is vested, by the Constitution, in the President.

" The President shall be Commander-in-Chief of the Army and Navy of the United States, and of the Militia of the several States, when called into the actual service of the United States."*

---

* Article II. Section 2.

The President, then. is a proper authority,—not, indeed, as President, but as Commander-in-Chief. As such he has legal power, by himself or through his subordinate officers, to take, and to destroy or to use, personal property belonging to the enemy. As such he is sole judge of the exigencies which render necessary such taking and such destruction or use.

In the exercise of this discretion he is not amenable under any provision of the Constitution. The Constitution, in making him commander-in-chief, neither designated nor restricted his powers as such; but it conferred upon him, by implication, all the powers appertaining, by the usage and law of nations, to that office. Strictly speaking, the only constitutional question which can be raised in this connection is as to whether the person so taking and destroying enemies' property was, at the time, legally commander-in-chief.

He is responsible for the manner of exercising this power under the law of nations; and, as the law of nations is to be construed in the interests of humanity and civilization, he is responsible in case his acts should outrage these great Christian principles. Humanity forbids us to lay waste a country, to sack towns and villages, to burn or pillage dwellings, to destroy public edifices not military. Humanity bids us respect the private property of non-combatant enemies, so far as this is compatible with the exigencies of war. If a commander-in-chief violate these rules, which civilization, in its progress, has dictated, it is an offence, not against the Constitution, but against international law. The legality of his acts may be called in question, not their constitutionality.

What was the manner in which the President, as commander-in-chief, took and cancelled the claims to involuntary labor owned by inhabitants of the insurrectionary States?

On the 25th of July, 1862, in pursuance of the sixth section of the act of July 17, 1862, commonly called the "Confiscation Act," the President issued a proclamation warning all insurgents to return to their allegiance within sixty days, on pain of certain forfeitures and seizures.

This warning proving ineffectual, the President, when the sixty days' notice had expired, issued a second proclamation, declaring that the slaves held within any State which, on the 1st of January then succeeding, should still be in rebellion against the United States, "shall be then, thenceforth, and forever free."

On the 1st of January, 1863, "by virtue of the power in him vested as Commander-in-Chief of the Army and Navy of the United States," he declared certain States, —namely, Arkansas, Texas, Louisiana, Mississippi, Alabama, Florida, Georgia, South Carolina, North Carolina, Virginia,—certain parishes in Louisiana and certain counties in Virginia excepted,—to be then in rebellion against the United States; and he further declared that all slaves in the said ten States, with the exceptions aforesaid, "are, and henceforward shall be, free."

In the last-mentioned proclamation the President recites that it is issued "in time of actual armed rebellion against the authority and government of the United States;" and, further, that Emancipation is declared "as a fit and necessary war-measure for suppressing said rebellion."

The number of claims to involuntary labor which this proclamation declared to be cancelled was about three millions. The forfeiture, under the war-power, of so great an amount of property, the cancelling of so vast a number of claims, disturbing, as it must, the

social and commercial elements throughout a large and
populous country, requires, for its justification, an object commensurate in grandeur with the magnitude of
the measure itself.

What was that object?

"All that a man hath," we are told, "will he give
for his life." And this is as true of nations as of individuals. No higher or greater object can be proposed
to any people than the maintenance of its national
unity, which is its national life.

At the time when the President, as commander-in-
chief, issued his Proclamation of Emancipation, the
life of the nation was imminently threatened.

A civil war, of proportions more gigantic than any
which history records, had been raging in our country
for more than a year and a half. The contending
parties had put into the field upwards of a million of
combatants. We of the North had already expended,
or contracted to expend, full a thousand millions of
dollars. The war had been carried on with varying
success,—now the Federal arms triumphant, now the
Confederate. Northern councils were divided, and
there was a loud clamor for peace, on terms the ac-
ceptance of which could but result in perpetual war.
So far as foreign nations had declared themselves,
either by official acts or by the expression of public
opinion, it appeared to be rather in favor of the
Southern insurgents than of the established Government. The contest had, till then, assumed no higher
character than that of one portion of a great nation
striving to secede from the main body of the same and
establish a separate independence ; and, in an effort of
that character, if no higher principle be involved, the
sympathy of the world is usually with the weaker
party.

In such a conjuncture, the best and wisest among us saw before them a protracted war, a doubtful issue. The bravest confessed to themselves that we had need of all our resources, even to the uttermost, in order to avert the breaking up of the great American Union into such petty, discordant sovereignties as are to be found in more southern portions of our hemisphere; into belligerent fragments, with the standing and influence, perhaps, of Venezuela or Costa Rica, of Nicaragua or Ecuador.

We had need of all our resources, even to the uttermost. Had we at that time employed them all? Had we not, up to that time, left in the hands of our enemies, with scarcely an effort to disturb it, one of the chief elements of their military strength?—nay, an element so overwhelmingly influential in its practical results, that, according to its management, against us or in our favor. might be the ultimate issue of the war, —defeat if we neglected it, victory if we improved the opportunity? Let us look closely to this.

By the census of 1860, the number of white males between the ages of eighteen and forty-five was, in the loyal States, about four millions; in the disloyal States, about a million three hundred thousand,—let us say, about three to one. The disparity seems great; but, as a basis of military strength, the calculation is wholly fallacious; for the disloyal States contained, when the insurrection broke out, three millions and a half of people* who were not insurgents. who did not voluntarily assist in the rebellion. but who were compelled by force to render it most efficient aid.

Out of the above four millions, the North had to pro-

---

* The eleven States who passed ordinances of secession contained, by the census of 1860, three millions five hundred and twenty-one thousand one hundred and ten slaves.

vide soldiers and (with inconsiderable exceptions, not usually extending to field-labor) laborers also.

Not so in the South. Her million three hundred thousand had more than their own number to aid them in military as well as agricultural labor; for, as among slaves both sexes are employed, from an early age to a late period of life, in the field, the number of laborers out of three millions and a half of slaves may fairly be put at two millions. Let us estimate three hundred thousand of these as employed in domestic service and other occupations followed by women among us, and we have seventeen hundred thousand plantation-hands, male and female, each one of whom counts against a Northern laborer on farm or in workshop, or a Northern soldier laboring on intrenchment or fortification; each one of whom, staying at home to labor, liberates a white man for active military duty in the field.

To one million three hundred thousand add one million seven hundred thousand, and we have three millions as the total, in the insurgent States, of numerical force available in this war; that is, of soldiers to fight and laborers to support the nation while fighting.

Then, supposing the negroes all loyal to their masters, or at least remaining to labor for them, the comparative military strength, so far as it is indicated by population, was as four in the North to three in the South.

If we take into account the fact that ours were the invading and attacking forces, while the insurgents had the advantage of acting upon their own territory, near to their supplies, with short inside lines of communication, and on the defensive, it need not surprise us that, after the lapse of a year and eight months of unintermitting war, the scale still remained in the balance, neither side yet hopelessly depressed.

Under such a condition of national affairs, when there was question of claims, held by the enemy, upon which rested his powers to supply his armies with the necessaries of life, it was incumbent upon us to go much further than to inquire whether the commander-in-chief had the right to take, and declare forfeited, these claims. The true and fit question is, whether, without a flagrant violation of official duty, he had the right to refrain from taking them.

"You have no oath," our present Chief Magistrate said, addressing, in his Inaugural, the insurgents already in arms against lawful authority,—"you have no oath registered in heaven to destroy this Government; while I have the most solemn one to preserve, protect, and defend it."

Can we suppose a grosser violation of that solemn oath, than would have been the failure to employ the appropriate means, sanctioned by the law of nations, gradually to withdraw from the enemy half his military strength? Has a President done his best to preserve the Government, to protect the people, until he shall have done this? Charged with the lives of millions, with the putting down of a gigantic rebellion and the restoring of tranquillity to the land, what right had our commander-in-chief, in the hour of utmost need, to scorn a vast element of war-strength placed within his reach and at his disposal? And, if he had refused to avail himself of such an element, would he not have been righteously held responsible for the hopes he blighted and the lives he cast away?*

---

* In this argument I have confined myself, in terms, to the proclamation of the President as authority sufficient to make Emancipation in the insurrectionary States legal and irrevocable. The argument, however, is equally applicable to the Acts of Congress on this subject; which acts have, besides, other grounds of validity, unnecessary here to recite.

Under such a state of things, it was eminently and
imperatively the duty of the President, "as a fit and
necessary war-measure for suppressing the rebellion,"
to declare free all the slaves held by the enemy in the
insurrectionary States, not merely to emancipate those
among them who might succeed in making their escape
and coming within our military lines. The important
and legitimate object was to present to those still held
in duress a strong and proper motive to sever all connection with the insurgents, to abstain from giving aid
and comfort to the insurrection, and to seek refuge
from the superior force which compelled them to give

The chief provision by Congress is contained in the ninth section of the
Act of July 17, 1862, commonly called the "Confiscation Act," as follows:—

"That all slaves of persons who shall hereafter be engaged in rebellion
against the Government of the United States, or who shall give aid or
comfort thereto, escaping from such persons and taking refuge within the
lines of the army: and all slaves captured from such persons or deserted
by them and coming under the control of the Government of the United
States; and *all slaves of such persons found or being within any place occupied by rebel forces and afterwards occupied by forces of the United States,*
shall be deemed captives of war, and shall be forever free of their servitude, and not again held as slaves."

By the decision of the Supreme Court, already cited, *all* the inhabitants
of the insurrectionary States are, in law, persons "engaged in rebellion;"
therefore all refugee slaves from insurrectionary States are, by this statute,
declared free.

Further, as all the insurrectionary States have been "occupied by rebel
forces," and as we may reasonably conclude that, if we prevail against the
South, all these States not already "occupied by forces of the United
States" will hereafter be so occupied, it follows that, by the operation of
this law, all the slaves in the insurrectionary States, even if no Emancipation Proclamation had ever been issued, would, before the end of the
war, have probably been entitled to freedom.

Strictly in the spirit of the above statute, and going only so far beyond
it as to declare slaves in portions of the insurrectionary States not yet
"occupied by forces of the United States" to be free in advance of such
occupation, was the President's action in the premises.

such aid and comfort, by fleeing to that portion of the country where lawful authority prevailed.

Another great principle is involved. Every publicist of repute has set forth (what common sense suggests), as among the most important of national rights and duties, the rule that a nation—especially a nation engaged in war—ought to protect itself not only against immediate, but against prospective, dangers. Deriving all rights attendant on conquest "from justifiable self-defence," Vattel says,—

"When the conqueror has subdued a hostile nation, he may, if prudence so require, render her incapable of doing mischief with the same ease in future. * * * If the safety of the State lies at stake, our precaution and foresight cannot be extended too far. Must we delay to avert our ruin till it has become inevitable? * * * An injury gives a right to provide for our future safety, by depriving the unjust aggressor of the means of injuring us."*

If, then, any of our enemy's possessions have been the special agency by which he has been enabled to injure us; if such possessions will still afford him the means to "do us mischief with the same ease in the future;" if thereby "the safety of the State lies at stake;" is it not an imperative duty to extend our precaution and foresight into coming years? Are we not bound by every consideration of enlightened statesmanship to "deprive our unjust aggressor of the means of injuring us" hereafter?

The case has not yet been fully stated. Not only have these possessions in our enemies' hands been the very sinews of war, but they were the original cause of the insurrection itself. The insurgents themselves,

---

* Vattel, Book III. § 201, 44, 45.

who best know their own motives, tell us this. One of
the most honest and intelligent among them, selected as
their Vice-President,—Alexander H. Stephens,—speaking for them before a vast audience at Savannah, a few
days after his election, publicly said,—

"Negro slavery was the immediate cause of the late
rupture and present revolution. Jefferson, in his forecast, had anticipated this, as the rock upon which the
old Union would split."

These possessions have caused one rebellion. Shall
they remain in the hands of the insurgents to cause
another? Can they remain in such hands without a
certainty of that very result? In other words, can we
reconstruct the Republic half free and half slave, yet
preserve, under the operation of these conflicting labor-
systems, permanent peace? Let us take a practical
view of this.

Alexander H. Stephens, adverting, in the address
already quoted from, to slavery, as having been regarded by the leading Revolutionary statesmen to be
"wrong in principle, socially, morally, and politically,"
says, "This stone, which was rejected by the first
builders, is become the chief stone of the corner in our
new edifice." And he adds, "Slavery is the natural
and moral [normal?] condition of the negro. This our
new government is the first in the history of the world,
based upon this great physical, philosophical, and moral
truth."*

This is the creed, self-expounded by its advocates,
which is professed by the Southern slaveholder. Con-
cede its truth, and South Carolina's Declaration of In-
dependence† is a document stamped with forecast, and

---

* Address of Alexander H. Stephens, already quoted. See Putnam's
Rebellion Record, vol. i., Documents, p. 45.

† "Declaration of Causes which induced the Secession of South Caro-

entitled to commendation. Whoever drafted it ran out
his premises to their logical results. The convention
that adopted it saw their way before them, and did not,
like their weak sympathizers in the North, expect in-
compatibilities.

Having set up their "great philosophical truth," the
corner-stone of their political system, they saw clearly
that they must insure it respect, that they must protect it from attack or condemnation; and they perceived
that this could not be done if they maintained fellowship with the North. "The non-slaveholding States,"
they declare, "have denounced as sinful the institution
of slavery." This, from citizens of the same Republic,
they cannot permit; nor, except by secession from the
non-slaveholding States, can they prevent it. "All
hope of remedy,"—thus their Declaration concludes,—
"all hope of remedy is rendered vain by the fact that
public opinion at the North has invested a great political
error with the sanctions of a more erroneous religious
belief."

Wise, in their generation, were South Carolina and
the States that followed her lead! Building their system of government upon a "great philosophical and
moral truth," which (unfortunately, they will say) the
rest of the civilized world still regards as a flagrant
moral falsehood, they can maintain the stability of their
political edifice only by debarring all questions, all discussions, that might assault and endanger its foundations. As in despotic monarchies it was found necessary
to declare it to be treason, punishable as a capital offence,
to question the right divine of kings, so in a slave empire they see it to be indispensable to forbid, on pain

lina," adopted Dec. 21, 1860. See Putnam's Rebellion Record, vol. I.,
Documents, pp. 3, 4.

of death, all opinions touching the sinfulness, or inconsistency with religion, of slavery.   Twenty-five years ago, they declared, from their places in Congress, that, in spite of the Federal Government, every abolitionist they caught should die a felon's death.*   It was no idle menace, as numerous murders for opinion's sake, committed in the South before the war, terribly attest.

Let us not blame the men, except it be for seeking to uphold the monstrous system handed down to them by their forefathers.   They *must* resist the Federal authority to maintain that system.   They *must* violate the constitutional provision which forbids to abridge " the liberty of speech or of the press:" self-defence and its necessities compel them.   They found this necessary before the war, in order to save slavery from destruction : the necessity will be increased beyond measure if slavery remain after its close.   Now that the President's Proclamation of Emancipation has stirred up, in every Southern plantation, the latent longing for freedom, the dangers to their slave-system from propagandism will be increased a hundredfold.

It follows that in this Republic, if reconstructed half slave, half free, no man known to be opposed in principle to slavery will be able to cross Mason and Dixon's line without imminent risk of life.   South of that line the constitutional provision touching the liberty of speech and of the press will remain inoperative.   A felon's death will await every resident or traveller in

---

* " Let an abolitionist come within the borders of South Carolina, if we can catch him, we will try him, and notwithstanding all the interference of all the governments on earth, including the Federal Government, we will hang him."—*Senator Preston, in debate in United States Senate, January*, 1838.

" If chance throw an abolitionist in our way, he may expect a felon's death."—*Senator Hammond, of South Carolina, in United States Senate,* 1836.

the South who prints or who utters, in public or in private, any denial that slavery is just and moral, any assertion that religion does not sanction it. The Constitution guarantees the right thus to print, thus to speak. The Federal Government is bound to maintain that constitutional right. But it *cannot* maintain it in a Republic half slave, half free. What then? *Slavery and the Constitution inviolate cannot coexist.* We must give up the one or the other.*

---

* Events have occurred among us here in the North, which, if it be painful, it is also useful, to recall, seeing that they serve as beacons to mark the dangers of the path we have been pursuing, and the incompatibility of slavery and free speech. Such an one was the burning, by a mob, twenty-eight years ago, in a free State, of a public building devoted to free discussion.

Pennsylvania Hall, a handsome public edifice situated in Sixth Street, near Cherry, Philadelphia, costing upwards of forty thousand dollars, was opened, before a respectable audience of three thousand persons, of whom the majority were ladies, on the 14th of May, 1838,—the managers announcing that it was dedicated to "free discussion of the principles of liberty and equality of civil rights." It continued open four days only, to crowded audiences throughout, the subjects discussed being slavery, the rights of the Indian, temperance, and requited labor. On the evening of the fourth day the building was destroyed.

I take the account of this act of vandalism from an official source,—the "*Report of the Committee on Police,*" read in Councils July 5, 1838 (Philadelphia, L. R. Bailey, 1838).

On the evening of the third day, May 16, while Angelina Grimke Weld was speaking, the "house was assaulted by a ruthless mob, who broke the windows, alarmed the women, and disturbed the meeting by yelling, stamping, and throwing brickbats and other missiles through the windows." (*Report*, pp. 15, 16.) No persons were arrested, "as an attempt to carry away the prisoners might lead to a successful rescue."

May 17th, the managers called upon the Mayor (John Swift) to "protect them and their property in the exercise of their constitutional right peaceably to assemble and discuss any subject of general interest." The Mayor (p. 17) said, "He could give them no assurance, if they persisted in their evening meetings, that the police was able to afford them adequate protection;" but "he would do all in his power."

In the evening before the meeting, he went up to the building, found a

But if we abandon the inviolability of the Constitution, if we attempt to perpetuate a state of things under which one of the most important provisions of the organic law which binds us together as a nation is habitually and openly outraged, if we surrender one of those sacred privileges to maintain which freemen first settled America,—a privilege the possession of which, more than of any one human right, distinguishes the citizen of a constitutional government from the subject of a despotism, a privilege which, beyond all others, is indispensable to human progress itself,—if we basely consent to such humiliation, can our Republic maintain either the respect of the world without or

---

crowd and a man haranguing them against the abolitionists, entered the Hall, and advised the managers not to hold their meeting. To this they assented, and the keys of the building were given up to the police. The Mayor returned home.

Later in the evening news was brought to him that an attack had commenced on the Hall. He collected a body of police and marched to the spot, "where the work of destruction was in rapid progress." He exclaimed to the crowd, "Is there nobody here to support the law?" But the only response was an assault on the police (p. 23). Two or three resolute men, who entered the building to protect it, were seized and ejected; the furniture was piled up and set on fire, and the crowd "directed the fire-engines not to play upon the Hall, or else their engines and hose would be destroyed" (p. 24). The building, with all it contained, was burned to the ground.

The feature in this case which indicates most strongly the dangerous influence of a perverted public opinion, is the feeble and apologetic tone in which the Report from which I have been quoting condemns the act. It speaks of Philadelphia as "having been selected as the rallying-point of men known among us only as restless agitators" (p. 14), and winds up thus:—"However excusable the excitement might be, it can never be tolerated without jeoparding our dearest rights" (p. 27).

All the details of the proceedings within the Hall, during its brief existence, showing that the speakers proposed reform through constitutional means only,—by "the ballot-box and petition,"—together with a full account of its destruction, will be found in a small volume entitled the "History of Pennsylvania Hall," Philadelphia, Merrihew & Gunn, 1838.

domestic tranquillity within? Certainly not. The North, now that her spirit is up, would not endure it for a moment. It would inevitably result in war.

Let us pass to another matter. In South Carolina's "Declaration of Causes" for secession, one of the chief (set forth as justifying and necessitating separation) is "the election of a man to the high office of President of the United States whose opinions and purposes are hostile to slavery." This, it is declared, the slave-holding States cannot permit, because, whenever it shall occur, "the Federal Government will have become their enemy."

To satisfy a slaveholding South so that she shall permit us again to unite with her, it is evident that we must do one of two things: either consent so to amend the Constitution that no man shall be eligible as President "whose opinions and purposes are hostile to slavery," or else make up our minds to a second insurrection the first time a President with such opinions happens to be elected. The constitutional amendment, our first alternative, would be an infamy, if it were a possibility; the second alternative is renewed war.

But the very head and front of our former offending against the South remains yet untouched,—the loose manner, to wit, in which she alleges that the fugitive-slave law has heretofore been enforced. This our offence was so grievous in the eyes of South Carolina that she put it forth in her Declaration as the first and in itself the all-sufficient cause for separation, adding, "Thus the constitutional compact has been deliberately broken, and South Carolina is released from her obligation."*

---

* Declaration of Causes, already quoted. Rebellion Record, vol. i., Documents, p. 4.

What chance, even the remotest, is there that, with Slavery and Freedom in political partnership, this rock of offence will be avoided hereafter? Let us for a moment imagine that the Emancipation Proclamation had no force in law. Nevertheless, it has been promulgated; its glad tidings have penetrated to the remotest haunts of Southern slavery. To the slave it is a reality. In his heart it has called up the assurance—the fervent hope, at least—that, if he can but once elude the vigilance of his master, there is yet freedom for him on this side of the grave. That hope once awakened throughout the length and breadth of the insurrectionary States, can it ever again be put to rest? Is it not certain that under its promptings—no matter how firmly we might re-establish slavery by law—these bondmen would cross the border by thousands, for hundreds that have sought refuge among us till now? And when they do pass into that land whose President proclaimed them free men, and where twenty abolitionists are to be found now for every one who was there on the day Fort Sumter fell, will there be increased cheerfulness, greater willingness to aid in their rendition, than there was before the war began? What a mockery is the question! On what a foundation of quicksand do they build, who found their hopes of future peace on the expectation that a fugitive-slave law will be more stringently enforced in the future than in the past,—on the vain dream that Northern spirit, whether flushed with victory or maddened by defeat, will find no occupation more noble than to pursue and secure poor fugitives deluded by a national promise basely broken, and who had been urged to flight by belief in our humanity and confidence in our truth!

In such a state of feeling, under such a state of things, can we doubt the inevitable results? Shall we escape border raids after fleeing fugitives? No sane man will expect it. Are we to suffer these? We are disgraced. Are we to repel them? It is a renewal of hostilities.

Turn which way we will, *slavery is war.* There is—in the very nature of things there can be—no security for peace or loyalty from a Slave State. The only practicable road to domestic tranquillity open to us now is through Emancipation.

But, in deciding a matter of such vast gravity as this, it behooves us to look to our relations with foreign nations, as well as to those between our own States.

That slavery is an element of weakness in war was denied three years ago by those Northern men who were in the habit of regarding it as a sacred thing, which to touch, even in an enemy's hands, was profane. No statesman will deny it now. The rebellion will be put down: through the clouds of war we see already the beginning of the end. But if the three millions of slaves, gradually coming over to us and swelling the ranks of our liberating armies, had been three millions of free men, loyal to the South,—if the population of the Southern States, without regard to color, had been a unit in this struggle,—should we have defeated them in their effort for recognition? If history speak truth, we should not. Never, since the world began, did nine millions of people band together, resolutely inspired by the one idea of achieving their independence, yet fail to obtain it. It is not a century since one-third of the number successfully defied Great Britain.

The present is teaching, and the future will teach more clearly yet, that slavery is an element of military weakness. We have taught that lesson to Europe. In case of foreign war, with slavery still existing among us, will she fail to remember and to apply it? In such a case, will England, will France, will any European

Power, save, perhaps, lagging Spain, respect an institution which they all regard as a national crime,—a crime for which many of them have atoned by repentance and at heavy cost? In the case of foreign hostilities, would not Lord Dunmore's proclamation* be reproduced in a far more dangerous form, with a far more fatal effect?

It is certain that it would. But this is the least of our dangers in such a contingency. In case of a foreign war, with master and slave still constituting a portion of our population, with whom will the masters side?—with us, the detested Yankees, or with those European potentates, all-but publicly invited already to forgive the undutiful doings of 1776 and to send a royal scion to reign over them?† Like causes continued produce like results. If we subdue the slave-masters, leaving them slave-masters still, can we expect that they will abstain from plotting foreign war that they may gain by it? And if they succeed in the treasonable plot, can we suppose that they will refrain from seeking their own advantage by an alliance with the enemy?

If we expose ourselves to these dangers, patent to common sense, we shall deserve our fate. To foreign as well as to domestic tranquillity, the only practicable path is through general Emancipation.

In other words, as we would hasten, by every lawful

---

* In this well-known document, after declaring against all persons who failed to resort to His Majesty's standard, " forfeiture of life and confiscation of lands," Lord Dunmore proceeds, "And I do hereby further declare all indented servants, negroes, or others (appertaining to rebels), free, that are able and willing to bear arms, they joining His Majesty's troops as soon as may be, for the more speedily reducing this colony to a proper sense of their duty to His Majesty's crown and dignity."

The proclamation was dated November 7, 1775.

† See note on page 126 (chapter on Slavery), *ante*,—being the testimony, as to this matter, of William Howard Russell.

and proper means, the advent of peace; as we would obtain, before this contest closes, a guaranty against its renewal; as we would protect ourselves, by prudent foresight and precaution, against foreign complications involving dismemberment of the nation,—and what duties, during war, more imperative than these?—we must take and cancel our enemies' claims to service and labor.   That service feeds our enemy; that labor supplies his commissariat.   Deprived of it, his power to injure us is taken from him; possessed of it, he remains our enemy—dangerous in peace, still more dangerous in war—while grass grows and water runs.

Is not the grandeur of the object, then, commensurate with the magnitude of the remedy?   If that remedy produce temporary disturbance of social and political elements throughout half our country, is not the alternative the dismemberment of that country itself,—its loss of unity, its loss of peace, its final decline and fall as one of the great Powers of the world?

So far, the argument has been one of policy alone; selfish, in one sense, it may be called, since it takes into account the interests of one only out of the two races which inhabit our country; an argument, too, sound and unanswerable if it be, which does not reach the full dignity of the subject, since it has not treated it in its relation to the progress of civilization and humanity, and to the national honor, ever intimately connected with the national life.

Opinions adverse to the lawfulness of slavery have, for a century past, been spreading and swelling into action throughout the civilized world.   They have taken practical form and shape,—they have become law,—till not a nation in Europe, Christian or Mohammedan, Spain alone excepted, stands out against them.

England led the way. In 1834 she emancipated all her slaves. King Oscar of Sweden followed her example in 1846; then came Denmark, in 1847; France, in 1848; Portugal, in 1856; the vast empire of Russia, in 1862; finally, with nearly thirty years' experience in English colonies and fifteen years' experience in those of France before her eyes, plain, practical, unimaginative Holland, by a vote in her Chambers of forty-five to seven, gave freedom, with compensation, to her forty-five thousand slaves; liberating them on the 1st of July last.

The opinions which gave rise to these national acts are gradually finding place among the maxims of international law, as expounded by modern commentators. Phillimore, a reputable authority, says:—

"There is a kind of property which it is equally unlawful for States as for individuals to possess,—property in man. A being endowed with will, intellect, passion, and conscience cannot be acquired and alienated, bought and sold, by his fellow-beings, like an inanimate or unreflecting and irresponsible thing. The Christian world has slowly but irrevocably arrived at the attainment of this great truth. * * * The black man is no more capable of being a chattel than the white man. The negro and the European have equal rights. Neither are among the 'res positæ in commercio' in which it is lawful for States or individuals to traffic."*

The United States, prompt, in other matters, to take part with the foremost and freest nations in asserting the principles of liberty and human rights, have lagged behind Europe on the subject of negro emancipation.

The chief reason is that a regard for law conflicted

---

* Commentaries upon International Law, by Robert Phillimore, M. P., London, 1853, vol. i. p. 316.

with a regard for liberty. To the American citizen the
Constitution stands in the place occupied, under the
monarchical system, by the sovereign in person. It is
the highest object of his loyalty. His veneration for
that instrument went so far as to influence his percep-
tions of justice. A majority in the North have always
held it to be a great wrong that human beings and their
descendants forever should be held in bondage. Up to
the time when this war made the slaveholders in eleven
States our enemies, we acquiesced in that wrong, lest,
in the endeavor to remedy it, greater evils might follow.
Though it be true that, before the war, the legality of
the slaveholder's claim to service or labor was denied,
on humanitarian grounds, yet a construction of the
Constitution adverse to such denial, and acquiesced in
by the nation throughout two generations, was held
by most men to be sufficient reason why the claim in
question should be regarded as private property and
respected as such. The majority held to the opinion
that it could not be taken except by a violation of the
Constitution,—in other words, by a revolutionary act.
They felt that though revolutionary acts become a justifiable remedy upon great occasions, as in 1776, yet
they are usually replete with peril; that it is easy to
pass the limit of regulated authority, but impossible
to estimate the dangers we may encounter when that
guardian limit is once transgressed.

That, in the minds of many Northern men, cupidity,
excited sometimes by supposed commercial advantages,
sometimes by selfish political calculations, came in aid
of constitutional scruple, may not be denied; and, so
far as that motive prevailed, our complicity, as a people,
is without palliation. But cupidity, commercial or political, was not the dominant motive; nor, but for the
restraint of the Constitution, would sordid considera-

tions have prevented the nation from shaking off the incubus which oppressed it.

Slavery, therefore, moral wrong as it is, was tolerated by the majority as one of the articles in a great national compromise which it was unlawful and perilous to violate. If, before the South had trampled under foot compromise and Constitution, those who directed the Federal Government, taking the initiative, had striven to eradicate the growing evil, the effort would have been vain; for they could not have carried the people with them. To human eyes there seemed, in this generation at least, no way out.

But God, who overrules evil for good, opened the way. They, the chief architects of the Great Wrong of the age, in whose hands alone seemed to have been left the power to hasten its downfall, have madly persisted in the very course that is leading, swiftly and inevitably, to that result. In the early stage of the war, Congress and the President proposed, and the majority of the nation expected, as the issue of this contest, a mere rehabilitation, with Southern laws and Southern institutions reacknowledged in their pristine form. In this the President and the North were sincere. Again and again warning was given, and the return of the insurgents to their loyal duty on these conditions was urged upon them. But their hearts were hardened, and they would not. By their obstinate perversity they closed the door against themselves. They persevered in their conspiracy against public law until Emancipation became an imperative measure of self-defence. They persevered until public opinion, revolutionized, demanded that measure as the only sure guaranty in the future for national safety and national peace. They, the slaveholders, became the abolitionists of slavery. Let us not take credit to ourselves for generous philanthropy. The South, reckless and blind, was herself the unwitting agent. And thus, in the providence of God, the very effort, by armed treason, to perpetuate an abuse has given us at once the will and the right to effect its eradication.

The time has come when it is constitutional to redress that abuse. No law restrains us. Henceforth we are responsible if, in the race for human freedom, we lag, with Spain, behind the rest of the civilized world. Henceforth we are responsible, before God and man, if, having at last become free to carry out in practice the noble declaration of our forefathers, that life, liberty, and the pursuit of happiness are among the inalienable rights of man, we basely refuse or neglect to do so.

We have a greater responsibility still. We are as one having an oath upon his soul. The maxim is well known that he who legally acts by another is himself the actor. The legal acts of the President are the acts of the nation. It was the people of the United States who, on the first day of January, eighteen hundred and sixty-three, set free three millions of men.

The deed is done,—lawfully, righteously done. Its validity is as well established as that of any other public act.

But to establish its validity is to establish the *status*, as freeman, of every person that was held as a slave, in the insurrectionary districts named, on the first day of the year eighteen hundred and sixty-three, whether he shall have physically escaped from bondage or not. "All persons held as slaves" within these districts are the words. Is the deed valid? The words stand. Is it invalid? It cannot free a single slave.

The argument, therefore, is unavailing that many of these people are still worked as slaves by persons setting at defiance the constitutional jurisdiction and the national will. A law set at defiance for the time is not thereby abrogated. In disturbed times, cases of illegal detention frequently occur. Such are these cases. But, in the eye of the law, the persons thus illegally detained have the rights of freemen, and the radical bayonet must enforce these rights.

Equally unavailing is the allegation that, as the Proclamation was but a war-measure, and therefore of force and virtue commensurate only with the war, its operation will cease when the immediate necessity which caused and justified it ceases,—that is, when peace is restored.

The exigency is as great in peace as in war. There are moral and national, as well as physical, necessities. "America," said the great Earl of Chatham during a memorable debate in the House of Lords in 1770, "was settled upon ideas of liberty."* In these ideas it was that our fathers founded the Republic. In these ideas alone can we, their descendants, maintain it.

The political necessity that nevermore, within these United States, shall life-long claims to service and labor be held by inhabitants thereof, will be as great when peace returns as it is now while war rages. Always morally unjust, this property has shown itself to be nationally dangerous. But a species of property that endangers the safety of a nation must not be left in the hands of its citizens, whether in peace or war.

Nor can it be pleaded that the taking of this property, vast as is its amount, is an act committed regardless of mercy to the vanquished, an act of harsh

---

* W. S. Johnson's Report of Chatham's Speech, in his letter to Governor Trumbull, of Connecticut, January 10, 1770; quoted by Bancroft in his History of the United States, vol. vi. p. 323.

severity, much less a deed of plunder,—no, nor yet a measure of punishment. Far from offending against any principle of humanity in destroying such property,—in other words, in cancelling life-long claims to service and labor,—the inhumanity would have been to refrain from destroying it.

Nor do we harm the slave-claimant, but greatly benefit him, by cancelling these claims. In point of fact, it is incalculably to his advantage—socially, pecuniarily, politically—to be without them. While he retains them, there will be between him and us a lack of the conditions necessary to a true union; there will be no loyal, concurrent sentiment of citizenship. But a forced union of States without the conditions under which alone concurrence of ideas and affections is possible, would be a measure unworthy of a statesman. Slaveholders and freemen can never, in these States, act together in friendship again. Therefore, for his own sake, the slaveholder must cease to be such.

Are we impertinently interfering in his business——arrogantly and improperly assuming to judge what is best for him—when we determine this? Not at all. The business is emphatically our own; for it intimately concerns our national existence. In deciding it as we see fit, there is neither impropriety nor arrogance, but proper precaution and prudent foresight. If he had refrained from levying war against his government, he would have had the right to judge and to act in this affair. As it is, he has lost it; and we have now the right and the power to decide the matter, not he.

But, in the second place, our power is restricted to the abrogation of these claims, and it ceases there. As a trust for a special object is exhausted with the execution of that object, so is the authority of the President, being in the nature of a trust, in this case. His object was to restore and render stable the national unity. To effect that great object—to preserve from permanent dismemberment the country over which he presides—he enfranchised three millions of its inhabitants. Under this act of his, third parties took vested rights. Under the inducements of this act of his, third parties took refuge within our lines, enlisted in our armies, fought in our battles. We had a right to confer these vested rights; we had a right to present these inducements; we had a right to accept this aid. But, having done all this, we have no right to resume what we have granted. We had a right to act: we have no authority to revoke our action. To enslave is not a power under the Constitution. No officer or department of the Government can exercise it. From that stain, at least, we are free. Were it otherwise, our Government would be the scorn of the age, a disgrace to Christendom.*

We have lost, by our own solemn act, the right henceforth to talk of reconstruction with the "peculiar institution" of the South left intact. Such language is now but a mischievous mystification. If the South conquer, she may, by superior force, hold as slaves those who, by our laws, are free men. But, for us, there *is* no longer, in any of the insurrectionary

<hr>

* That the Supreme Court of the United States has no right to sit in judgment upon, or to reverse, a great measure of national policy, is as certain as that the powers of that court are judicial, not legislative. We do not argue this point at length here, because it comes up more appropriately in the chapter treating of the constitutionality of Emancipation in the loyal Slave States. There the argument will be found at length, with references to the decisions of that court itself which bear upon this subject.

States, a peculiar institution to be left intact. We may build up anew that institution, in violation of law, it is true,—for neither the President nor Congress nor any judicial tribunal in the land has any more authority to consign a freedman to slavery than they have to hang him without crime or trial,—but we may build it up if we have power enough, or connive at it if we are shameless enough, just as a highwayman may seize a purse, or a burglar carry off a basket of silver-ware.

Whether, when we shall have suffered vanquished Treason to dictate her own terms; whether, when we shall have stooped to purchase—not peace, for God's best blessing cannot be so purchased—but a worthless truce, as brief as treacherous, by an act of usurpation that assumes to sign away the liberties of three millions of free people;—whether, when we shall have done this great thing, we shall have any right to set up for more honest or more virtuous than the felon trader who makes a midnight descent on the Congo coast and steals thence three or four hundred wretches to crowd the hold of his slave-ship,—that will be a question to be settled, at our leisure, with our own consciences.

"The way of the transgressor is hard." It is better to lose fortune than fair fame; and national disgrace is worse than national disaster. A convict, when he is known and remembered as such, may, because of the stain that attaches to him, toil faithfully through half a lifetime ere men take him again by the hand. And a people, stamped by their own public records as lawless and forsworn, may travel a long and a weary road —a reproach, the while, and a byword among nations —ere they can take an honored stand once more among the civilized Powers of the earth.

In concluding this branch of the subject, I briefly group together the propositions that have been advanced.

The inhabitants of the insurrectionary States are, in contemplation of law, without exception, public enemies.

Property belonging to an enemy may, by the law of nations, be seized by the proper military authority and appropriated or destroyed.

In like manner, claims or debts due by a public enemy to an inhabitant of this country may be seized and cancelled.

The claims to service or labor upon which rests negro slavery are, in contemplation of the Constitution, in the nature of debts or *choses in action*, and may, when held by an enemy, be declared null and void.

These claims, because of the labor which they command, constitute a chief resource of the insurgents for carrying on the war, and therefore essentially tend to protract it; for which reason it was the duty of the commander-in-chief to take and cancel them.

The interests growing out of these claims have been the cause of the present insurrection, and there can be no sufficient guaranty for peace while they exist; for which reason also it becomes a duty to declare them null and void.

These claims involve a great moral wrong which the insurrection has made it legal to redress; and we are now responsible, as a nation, if we fail to redress it by their abrogation.

The President's Proclamation of Emancipation was legal and righteous; it was the act of the nation, and cannot, lawfully, nor without violating the national faith, solemnly pledged, be revoked.

Therefore the emancipation of all the slaves in the insurrectionary portions of the Union was an act legal and irrevocable.

CHAPTER IV.

THE CONSTITUTIONALITY OF EMANCIPATION IN THE LOYAL SLAVE STATES.

As the slaveholders of the insurrectionary States, now at war with the United States, are public enemies, while the slaveholders of the Border or non-insurrectionary Slave States are friends, entitled to all the rights of citizens, the question touching the right to confiscate and cancel the claims to service and labor held by the former is essentially a different question, based on different principles, from the question whether we have a constitutional right to take and cancel the same class of claims held by the latter.

In the preceding pages it has been shown—

That slavery was the cause of the present insurrection.

That if slavery be suffered to continue in existence, it will remain a constant menace to the integrity of our Government, and an inevitable source of future war.

And that, therefore, prudence and foresight require that, for the sake of the national unity and national peace, slavery be forever abolished throughout these United States.

Though the military necessity be more urgent in the insurgent States, seeing that every slave taken or escaping from bondage is one laborer less to supply the enemy's commissariat, yet the general proposition is as true of the Border States as of those in rebellion. Indeed, fugitive-slave-law difficulties, of all others the most likely to bring on a war, would chiefly arise through refugees from Border States.

The slaves of disloyal owners in these States have already been emancipated by act of Congress. There remain in bondage, under State laws, certainly less than three-quarters of a million, scattered over a long narrow border-strip, bounded on the north by free States and on the south by States whence slavery has been legally banished, or else dotted in isolated parishes or counties intermixed with enfranchised slaves.

Can we maintain in perpetuity so anomalous a condition of things? Clearly not. At every step embarrassments innumerable obstruct our progress. No industry, no human sagacity, would suffice to determine the ten thousand conflicting questions that must arise out of such a chaos. Must the history of each negro be followed back so as to determine his *status*, whether slave or free? If negroes emancipated in insurrectionary States are sold as slaves into Border States, or into excepted parishes or counties, can we expect to trace the transaction? If slaves owned in Border States, or in excepted parishes or counties, are sold to loyal men in insurrectionary States, are they still slaves, or do they become free? Are we to admit or to deny the constitutionality of Border State laws which arrest, and imprison as vagrants, and sell into slavery to pay expenses of arrest and imprisonment, free negro emigrants from insurrectionary States?* But why multiply

---

* If, hereafter, Attorney-General Bates's decision, that a free negro is a citizen, be sustained by the Supreme Court, then, should the question come up before it, the State laws above referred to will be declared un-

instances? The longer this twilight of groping transition lasts, it will be only confusion the worse confounded.

To respect and to protect such a straggling remnant of slavery would be practically impossible, if it were desirable; and—aside from its being an old root of bitterness left in the ground to sprout and bear fruit in the future as it has borne fruit in the past—no freedman can be assured of his liberty while there remains a spot within the Union where he can be held as a slave.

If we would act as statesmen, having in view the peace and safety of our country through all future time, we must meet the great difficulty before us broadly, effectually, honestly, and in accordance with the dictates of Christianity and civilization. The demands of honor coincide with the conditions of safety. To satisfy both, we have a great duty to perform. It is to follow the noble example of England, and France, and Sweden, and Denmark, and Portugal, and Russia, and Holland. It is to enact, not merely that all persons held as slaves who happened, on the 1st of January, 1863, to be within certain insurrectionary limits, shall be free,—thus leaving a narrow belt of slavery to divide our country in two, and to separate the freed States of the South from the free States of the North,—it is not merely to carry out this fragmentary and imperfect scheme; it is not to do, for the cause of humanity, only what we cannot help doing; it is not merely to deprive the enemy in this present war of the means that augment his strength and enable him to protract the contest: it is, by taking a brave, bold stand for Human Liberty, irrespective of race or color, to lay deep and firm the foundations of

---

constitutional. But, meanwhile, they have not been so declared, and are in force.

The negro-excluding laws of Indiana and Illinois are in the same category.

that domestic tranquillity which endures from generation to generation only for those nations whose people
walk in the paths of justice and mercy, approved in the
sight of God and man.

It is to enact once and forever the emancipation of
every slave that treads the soil of the United States.
In the progress of this insurrectionary upheaval, we
have reached a point at which there is neither honorable
nor prudent alternative left.

Does any constitutional difficulty stand in the way?

The law or custom of all civilized nations, based on
considerations of public utility, authorizes the taking
of private property, with just compensation, for public
use, when important public interests demand it. We
are familiar with the operations of such a rule. When
a conflagration in a city threatens to spread far, houses
in the line of its progress may be seized and destroyed
by the authorities, in order to arrest it; and the owners
are not held to have been wronged, if they are paid
for such losses under an equitable appraisement. The
opening of a street in improving a city, the running
of a railroad, are held in this and other countries to
be objects of sufficient importance to justify what the
French law calls *"appropriation forcée pour cause d'utilité
publique."*

This principle is expressly recognized by the Constitution. In that instrument there is an admission of
the right to take private property, with just compensation made, for public use.* And it will not be argued
that a claim of one inhabitant of the United States to
the service of another, whether for a term of years or
for life, is a species of property which has been constitutionally exempted from such appropriation. It is

* Amendments to the Constitution, Article 5.

evident that, if a claim to the service of a slave cannot constitutionally be so taken and cancelled, neither can the claim to the service of an apprentice.

Thus the right to declare compensated emancipation in the United States is clear, provided important public interests demand it. But we have already shown that the public interests demanding such a measure, in this case, are the highest and the most vital that ever presented themselves to the councils of a nation.

The right referred to is vested in the National Legislature. If technical proof of this be demanded, it is to be found in a few brief propositions.

1. The Constitution (section 8) confers on Congress certain essential powers,—as, to collect taxes, without which no government can be supported.

2. The Constitution (same section) authorizes Congress to "make all laws that shall be necessary and proper for carrying into execution" these powers.

3. An insurrection, extending over eleven of the United States, prevents, throughout a considerable portion of the Union, the possibility of carrying into execution the essential powers thus granted to Congress.

4. Because of the resistance offered by the insurrectionary States to these constitutional powers, it becomes the duty of Congress to pass all laws that are necessary and proper not only, by successfully terminating the war, to enforce these powers in the present, but to secure their supremacy in the future,—in other words, to insure permanent obedience to the laws, thus averting anarchy.

All this will be conceded; but a question remains. Who is to judge what laws are necessary and proper to carry into execution the powers expressly conferred on Congress by the Constitution, and which are thus obstructed and defeated?

Or, to put directly the case in point : if Congress, sharing the deep conviction that has come over the nation as this contest proceeded, should reach the conclusion that there is no effectual means to secure, throughout the future, peaceful obedience to the laws, except the eradication of slavery, and should act accordingly, is such action constitutional and final? In the selection of the means to effect this constitutional object, is Congress the sole judge of their propriety and necessity? Or is the question as to the fitness of these means a judicial as well as a legislative question?

We must discriminate here. It would undoubtedly be competent for the Supreme Court, if the question came legitimately before it, to decide, in any special case, whether Congress has the right, under the Constitution, to take private property, with just compensation, for public use. That is a judicial question. But when a vast system of claims is to be thus taken for a great political end, when this is done as the only effectual means to preserve the integrity of the Union, or to bring a war to a successful issue, or to establish lasting peace, and when the matter to be decided is whether this taking *is* the most wise or appropriate means to secure these all-important objects,—that is a question of statesmanship, of governmental discretion, of political expediency, and, therefore, purely legislative. It is not competent for the Supreme Court to sit in judgment on the wisdom of a great measure of national policy.

Whenever the judicial branch of the Government assumes, and is permitted to exercise, such a power, the Government itself will be in the hands, not of the representatives of the people, elected by the people, but of a few men (at the present ten only) nominated by the President, confirmed by the Senate, and holding their offices for life. The trust which, by the Constitution, is committed to the personal judgment and discretion of the National Legislature, and for which the members of that Legislature are responsible only to their constituents, the people, will have been usurped by another branch of the Government, to which the Constitution assigns no such trust, grants no such discretion.

Nothing would be more radically subversive of our institutions than such a usurpation of jurisdiction. If it were consummated, we should be living under an oligarchy, not under a republic.

But we need be under no apprehension that it ever will be. The Supreme Court itself, speaking by the mouth of one of its most distinguished presiding officers, has expressly disclaimed the possession of any such authority.

In the well-known case of McCulloch against the State of Maryland,* Chief-Justice Marshall delivered the decision of the Supreme Court; and by that decision the following principles were established :—

1. The construction of the words "necessary and proper," as employed by the framers of the Constitution, in the above connection. The Chief-Justice says,—

"The term 'necessary' does not import an absolute physical necessity so strong that one thing to which another may be termed necessary cannot exist without that other."

2. As to the degree of the necessity which renders constitutional a law framed to carry a constitutional power into execution, the rule by this decision is,—

"If a certain means to carry into effect any of the powers expressly given by the Constitution to the

---

* February Term, 1819. 4 Wheaton's Rep., 316. Unwilling here to multiply words, I pray reference to the decision itself.

Government of the Union be an appropriate measure, not prohibited by the Constitution, the degree of its necessity is a question of legislative discretion, not of judicial cognizance."

8. But still more explicitly is the question answered, who is to be the judge of the appropriateness and necessity of the means to be employed, thus:—

"The Government which has a right to do an act, and has imposed upon it the duty of performing that act, must, according to the dictates of reason, be allowed to select the means."

Thus, then, the matter stands. The powers to lay and collect taxes, to exercise authority over forts and arsenals of the United States, to suppress insurrection, and various others equally essential, are expressly given by the Constitution to Congress. It is the right and duty of Congress to carry these powers into effect. In case of obstruction or defeat of existing laws framed to that intent, it is the right and duty of Congress to select such means and pass such additional laws as may be necessary and proper to overcome such obstruction and enforce obedience to such laws. These means must not be prohibited by the Constitution; but whether they are the most prudent or the most effectual means, or in what degree they are necessary, are matters over which the Supreme Court has no jurisdiction. As Chief-Justice Marshall has elsewhere in this decision expressed it, for the Supreme Court to undertake to inquire into the degree of their necessity, "would be to pass the line which circumscribes the judicial department and to tread on legislative ground."

There must, of course, be congruity or relevancy between the power to be enforced and the means proposed to enforce it. While Congress is to judge the degree of necessity or propriety of these means, they must not be such as to be devoid of obvious connection with the object to be attained.

In this case, the objects to be attained are the enforcement of the laws, the suppression of the rebellion, the restoration and preservation of peace, and the maintenance of the national unity.

But these laws are resisted, and this insurrection prevails, and the national unity is violated, in those States, and in those States only, in which the life-long claims to the service or labor of persons of African descent are held under State laws. In States where these claims are comparatively few,—as in Delaware, Maryland, Missouri,—disaffection only prevails; while in States where the number of slaves approaches or exceeds that of whites,—as in South Carolina, Alabama, Georgia,—insurrection against lawful authority is flagrant and outspoken; the insurrectionary acts of these States being avowedly based on the allegation that slavery is not safe under the present constitutionally-elected President, and that its permanent preservation can be insured by the disruption of the national unity alone.*

All this is matter of history. And there would be as much propriety in denying the connection between the sun and the light of day as that between slavery and the rebellion.

This point settled, nothing remains to be determined except the question whether, under existing circumstances, emancipation be or be not the policy most fitting and wise, the policy best calculated to assure, in the future, the peaceful execution of the law. And this, "according to the dictates of reason" (to repeat Chief-Justice Marshall's words), must be left to Con-

---

* The official proof of this assertion has already been furnished.

gress to decide. If Congress believes that Emancipation is no longer a question of sectional interference, but of national preservation, it has the right to judge, and the constitutional right to act upon that judgment. If Congress believes that, in order to enforce law and suppress insurrection, it is necessary and proper to take and cancel all claims to life-long service or labor held in the Slave States, and if claims to service or labor, whether for years or for life, held by one inhabitant of the United States against another, be a species of property not specially exempted by the Constitution from seizure for public use, then an act of compensated Emancipation is strictly constitutional.*

The substance of the argument here made amounts to this,—that, as to the claims to service or labor by persons of African descent held by inhabitants of insurrectionary States or by disloyal inhabitants of other States, it is lawful to confiscate and cancel them without compensation; while, as to such claims held by loyal men in non-insurrectionary States, it is legal to take them, making just compensation.

In other words, in the former case uncompensated Emancipation, in the latter compensated Emancipation, is in accordance with law and permitted by the Constitution.

That is the legal aspect. In a humanitarian view, Emancipation is one of the highest duties of Christian civilization.

---

* For a proposed form of an Act of General Emancipation, see Appendix, Note B.

PART III.

THE FUTURE OF THE AFRICAN RACE IN THE UNITED STATES.

"WERE the benefits of civilization to be partial, not universal, it would be only a bitter mockery and cruel injustice."—DUCHATEL.

PART III.

THE FUTURE OF THE AFRICAN RACE IN THE UNITED STATES.

CHAPTER I.

FOREBODINGS REGARDING THE FUTURE OF THE NEGRO.

AMONG the problems connected with the future of
our country, the destiny of the African race among us
is one of the most important. And on no other great
national question have more erroneous ideas prevailed,
both among ourselves and among those who have looked
on, even with favoring eyes, watching the progress of
our republican experiment.

There are evils so vast and radical that nothing short
of a bloody revolution has hitherto been found sufficient to extirpate them. So, the eradication of slavery
throughout a country containing four millions of slaves,
estimated by their masters as property worth twelve
or fifteen hundred millions of dollars. So,—a difficulty
greater still,—the eradication of that prejudice of race
and color which first suggested to the cupidity of white
men the exaction of forced labor from negroes, and has
ever since been fed and fostered through the influence
of the abuse to which it gave birth.

Such a revolution may bring about changes of national

opinion and national condition which wise and philosophical writers had pronounced to be beyond the limits
of possibility. Thus De Tocqueville, when, in his work
on American Democracy, he said,—

"To induce the whites to abandon the opinion they
have conceived of the moral and intellectual inferiority
of their former slaves, the negroes must change; but
as long as this opinion exists, they cannot change."*

This would make the future of the American negro,
free or slave, absolutely hopeless; but no absolutely
hopeless future exists, under the economy of God, in
this world of progress.

There never were sufficient reasons for saying this.
But to say it to-day would be far more inexcusable than
to have said it when De Tocqueville wrote. We have
gathered, during the vast upheavals of the last three
years, such experience as ages of undisturbed monotony
might fail to furnish. Events have occurred which no
human foresight could anticipate. Contingencies have
arisen which not only convulse our political world, but
stir to their foundations the social elements of society
around us.

The whites have changed, and are still rapidly changing, their opinion of the negro. And the negro, in his
new condition as freedman, is himself, to some extent,
a changed being. No one circumstance has tended so
much to these results as the display of manhood in

---

* Democracy in America, by Alexis de Tocqueville, Cambridge edition,
1862, vol. i. p. 459.

De Tocqueville's chapter on the black population of the United States is
one of the saddest and dreariest ever penned by a statesman. How just
his observation (p. 457) that "of all the ills which threaten the future of
the Union, the most formidable arises from the presence of a black population upon its territory"! He saw the impending danger. Is it strange
that, living when he did, he could not see the way out?

negro soldiers. Though there are higher qualities than strength and physical courage, yet, in our present stage of civilization, there are no qualities which command, from the masses, more respect.

But De Tocqueville could never have imagined, even as a remote possibility, the raising and equipping, in the United States, of a hundred thousand negro troops.

His anticipations turned in a different direction. He did not look forward to an insurrection of the whites against the Government: he predicted an insurrection of slaves against their masters. He predicted, further, that emancipation itself would not avert this catastrophe; but this last prediction was based upon the assumption that, free or slave, the whites would never accord to the blacks their rights as freemen. He says:—

"I am obliged to confess that I do not regard the abolition of slavery as a means of warding off the struggle of the two races in the Southern States. The negroes may long remain slaves without complaining; but if they are once raised to the level of freemen, they will soon revolt at being deprived of almost all their civil rights."*

If De Tocqueville's premises were just, we might admit his conclusion. We cannot expect, in a democratic republic, to maintain domestic tranquillity, if we deprive millions of freemen of their rights as such.

Public opinion may not, at the present time, have reached this conviction, but it is fast approaching it. Three-fourths of the States might not to-day, but ere long they will, pass some such amendment to the Constitution as this:—

"Slavery shall not be permitted, and no discrimina-

* Democracy in America, vol. i. p. 486.

tion shall be made, as to the civil or political rights of persons, because of color."

Whenever we shall have so amended the Constitution, the path before us will be plain and safe. But short of entire justice there is no permanent security.

CHAPTER II.

DO WE NEED THE AID OF THE NEGRO AS A LOYAL CITIZEN?

In the immediate exigencies of our present situation is to be found strong additional motive for such an act.

It would be, under any circumstances, a thing anomalous and repugnant to our system of government that four and a half millions of the governed, free citizens like the rest, should remain permanently taxed and not represented. But, aside from the essential injustice of this, its political results merit our gravest consideration.

At the close of the war, after the waste in battle of human life, and the further diminution in the South of her white population by emigration to Europe and to Mexico, the inhabitants of the insurrectionary portion of the Union will, we may assume, be nearly equally divided between the races. How will these inhabitants stand divided as to loyalty?

This is a question which it is impossible to answer with precision, except as to the colored people. They, with exceptions so rare that they are hardly worth taking into account, are all loyal,—as our commission, coming into contact with them in every portion of the Union where they can be reached, abundantly verified.

But in what state of mind will the close of the present

contest leave the vanquished? Not only as to those who engaged from the first heartily in the war, but as to that larger number whose sympathies, after the strife commenced, gradually became enlisted in what they called the cause of the South, inducing them to join the rebel ranks without compulsion,—can we seriously doubt the present state of their feelings towards us? Will these be less bitter if we quell this rebellion? Submission is not conversion. The sword conquers; it does not convince. Time alone can allay the wide-spread irritation which so embittered and protracted a struggle as this must needs leave behind it. And, meanwhile, to whom shall we be able to trust for re-establishment of order and maintenance of loyalty in the pacificated districts? To the Union men of the South, who, with their lives in their hands, resisted, through good and through bad report, the torrent of secession which inundated their land? Who can doubt their zeal and their courage? But what is their number? Is it a half, or a third, or a fourth, of the whole number of Southern whites?

The inevitable, doubtless, has great power over all men. From a hopeless cause there are numerous deserters. But will not many of these be weak and unreliable? And, when all are reckoned, will not two-thirds, three-fourths, remain only sullenly acquiescent?

All thoughtful men will give to such considerations much weight, and will acknowledge, with earnest anxiety, the difficulties that lie before us. They will admit it to be one of the great questions of the day, whether (leaving the abstract right or wrong of the case untouched) we can prudently or safely, for our own sakes, withhold from the freedman his political rights, and thus leave disfranchised, at a critical juncture in our history, a loyal half of a disturbed and dis-

affected population They will ask themselves whether,
as we have found need of the negro as a soldier to aid
in quelling the rebellion, we do not require his assistance as pressingly, in the character of a loyal citizen,
in reconstructing, on a permanently peaceful and
orderly basis, the insurrectionary States.

The doubt which naturally suggests itself in opposi-
tion is, not whether loyal votes are urgently needed,
but whether by admitting the freedman to suffrage we
may not seriously lower the average character of the
constituency which, under our democratic system, elects
to office State representatives, Congressmen, municipal
authorities, a President, and other subordinate magis-
trates, and whether by such a step we do not risk the
failure, or the degeneracy, of our republican system.

It will suggest itself that the negro, while in slavery,
was debarred from education, and that at this day few
of the freedmen can either read or write. In addition
to the ignorance resulting from this disability, we find
vices among slaves just freed, which appertain to their
former condition. Men who own no property do not
learn to respect the rights of property. Men who are
subjected to despotic rule acquire the habit of shielding
themselves from arbitrary punishment by lying. Men
who have never worked for themselves learn to shirk
work which is to enure solely to the benefit of others.
All this is to be taken into account. But with the
extirpation of the cause the effect gradually ceases.
In point of fact, it has been already found (as our commission satisfactorily verified) that the vices above
referred to are not deeply rooted, and that each may be
gradually eradicated by a proper appeal to the self-
respect of the newly-made freedman and by a strict
recognition of his rights. He is found quite ready to
copy whatever he believes are the obligations connected

with the rights of what he looks up to as the superior race, even if these prove a restraint upon the habits of license belonging to his former condition.   He is found willing, also, to work for moderate wages if promptly paid,* docile and easily managed, not given to quarrelling, of temperate habits, cheerful and uncomplaining if treated with justice and common humanity.

It should be remembered, too, in estimating his capacity to exercise political rights, that slavery had rendered him wary and suspicious.   The habit of the slave is, while assenting to whatever his master says, secretly to hold to his own opinion, and to act upon it whenever opportunity offers.   His sagacity is developed.   I do not think the freedman will be found a ready tool for the political demagogue.

Upon the whole, we shall find it difficult to bring any argument against recognizing the political rights of the negro which does not apply against the principle of universal suffrage itself.   Many regard the result of that principle as a practical failure, adducing in proof the fact that there are tens of thousands of voters among us incompetent and unworthy to act as such. Some have sought to obtain purity of elections by weeding out all foreign-born voters.   But if suffrage

---

* Captain Hooper, the acting superintendent at Port Royal under General Saxton, having charge of some seventeen thousand refugees, testified before our commission :—

Question.—" Do these people work willingly for wages?"

Answer.—"I never knew a case, where a colored man had reasonable security for getting wages,—even moderate wages,—that he was not willing to work."

Such cases, however, occur, as other witnesses testify; but the general rule, as we had abundant evidence to prove, is as Captain Hooper states it. Whenever we found complaints of idleness, or refusal to work, they were referable, in nine cases out of ten, to the fact that payment for labor was delayed for months, sometimes never made at all.

is to be restricted by qualification, we must seek some
stricter test of honesty and competence than the accident either of birth or of color.

Under ordinary circumstances, it would seem not
unreasonable that we should delay the recognition of
the freedman's right to suffrage for a time, until education and habits of freedom had prepared him to
exercise it. We might delay if domestic tranquillity
prevailed, if the loyalty of those States chiefly inhabited by the negro were unquestioned. We might
delay if we could dispense with his aid. But I am
able to make no reliable calculation according to which
we can dispense with it. When we shall first proceed
to reconstruction, one-third of all the white population
of the South is a full estimate for the proportion we
are likely to find honestly and earnestly disposed to
aid us in the work; that is, one-sixth only of the
entire population, white and colored. But can we
safely proceed to organize a republican government in
any country on the basis of one-sixth of its population?
Should we evince common sense in attempting to do so,
when we can have three-sixths more to aid that small
band of Southern loyalists in their arduous task?

God, who made the liberation of the negro the condition under which alone we could succeed in this war,
has now, in his providence, brought about a position of
things under which it would seem that a full recognition of that negro's rights as a citizen becomes indispensable to stability of government in peace.

In view of such considerations, it is difficult to resist
the conclusion that, before receiving back into political
fellowship the insurgent portions of the Union, it
should be legally established, as one of the principles
imperative in reconstruction, that all freemen shall
be legally secured in equal rights,—thus practically

carrying out the section of the Constitution which provides that the United States shall guarantee to every State a republican form of government.

From the observations made in various sections of our country which as a member of our commission it became my duty to visit, I do not believe that in accepting this necessary aid we incur risk of admitting into our system of government an element of deterioration.

CHAPTER III.

CAN THE NEGRO, AS FREEDMAN, MAINTAIN HIMSELF?

My own observations, together with the evidence obtained from persons having much experience among freedmen, justify the conclusion that the African race, as found among us, lacks no essential aptitude for civilization, yields willingly to its restraints, and enters with alacrity upon its duties. His personal rights as a freedman once recognized in law and assured in practice, there is little reason to doubt that the negro will become a useful member of the great industrial family of nations. Once released from the disabilities of bondage, he will somewhere find, and will maintain, his own appropriate social position.

What that precise position will be—whether we shall find a fair proportion of our colored population worthy competitors with whites in departments of art and science and literature—we have at this time no means of determining. The essential is, that the enfranchised negro is as capable of taking care of himself and his family as any other portion of our people.

On no one point have our commission found more con-
vincing testimony than on this.

In the cities of New Orleans, Washington, Balti-
more, Louisville, St. Louis, and elsewhere, we found a
numerous free colored population supporting themselves, under grievous and depressing disabilities,*
without any aid whatever even from those legal sources
appointed for the relief of indigent whites. They are
not admitted to almshouses. They obtain no county
or parish relief. Scarcely any beggars are found
among them. Like the Quakers, they maintain their
own poor. When a case occurs in which a family is
unable to meet the expenses of sickness, or perhaps
the cost of a funeral, it is among themselves alone
that a subscription-paper (usually called a "pony
purse") passes, in aid of the sufferers.

A striking incident, illustrative of this peculiarity
among them, came to the knowledge of our commission when visiting St. Louis. At the commencement
of the war there were about five thousand free colored
people in that city. During a portion of the years 1861
and 1862, in consequence of the disturbed condition

---

* Mr. James Speed, an eminent lawyer of Louisville, testified:—"We
have a law which makes it felony for a free negro to go out of the
State and return to it; but I have never known a conviction under it
here. I have heard of two prosecutions under it in another part of the
State of which one resulted in a conviction."—*Testimony taken in Kentucky,* p. 29.

Washington Spaulding (colored) deposed:—"The mother of a young
colored man, who lived here [in Louisville], moved across the river, and,
being on her death-bed, sent for him; but, on account of the law, he
could not go, and did not attend the funeral."—*Testimony taken in Kentucky,* p. 78.

Another law, equally oppressive, prevailing and enforced in Kentucky
and other Slave States, is, that no free colored man shall keep a store or
shop of any kind, or a tavern. What an unheard-of disability would a
white man consider such a prohibition as that!

of Missouri and the frequent raids which desolated that State, great distress prevailed, and many persons from the country, both white and colored, took refuge in St. Louis. Wages fell to twenty-five cents a day; and even at that low rate labor was scarce.

Under these circumstances, the suffering was so general that great exertions were made for its relief. For many months throughout these two years the city expended two hundred dollars a month to keep the unemployed from starving, and, in the winter season, from freezing. The Provident Association spent five thousand dollars; the Society of St. Vincent de Paul, ten thousand. Private individuals contributed largely. In the management of these various charities no discrimination was made as to color. The total number relieved was about ten thousand, and out of that number two persons only were colored. There were but two *applications* for relief from colored persons,—both women; one bed-ridden, the other a cripple. These facts were communicated to the commission by the Register of the city of St. Louis,—a gentleman who was himself one of the managers in the distribution of the relief-funds referred to.* The testimony of all the gentlemen concerned in the management of the various relief-societies was, he said, to the same effect,—that "the colored people asked for nothing."

The same was found true among the free negroes in Canada West, as was ascertained by one of the members of the commission who visited that country and took voluminous testimony as to the character and condition of the refugees who have settled there.†

---

* Testimony of R. A. Watt, City Register of St. Louis.—(Testimony taken by the Commission in Kentucky, Tennessee, and Missouri, pp. 145, 146.)

† Supplemental Report (A) on the Refugees in Canada West, pp. 60, 102.

It would be difficult to find stronger proof of the
ability and willingness of poor blacks to maintain
themselves than is shown in cases where they "hire
themselves," as it is called, and still pay their way.
We have given two examples of this in the chapter on
"Slavery;"* and they but represent hundreds of similar cases to be found in all the chief cities of the South.
In the one, it will be remembered, a mother paid two
hundred and sixty dollars a year to be allowed the privilege of supporting herself and two children by washing. What white washerwoman would like to undertake that? In the other case, a man and his wife paid
three hundred and seventy-two dollars a year, throughout eleven years, for permission to labor and to feed
and clothe their children until they were old enough
to work; and then they were taken from them. How
few white laborers would stand up at all under the
burden of such a capitation-tax! How few, under circumstances of such cruel discouragement, would have
maintained, as these two slaves did, a comfortable home,
tidily kept, and children clean, well clad, and thriving!

One hears current among slaveholders the assertion
that negroes, emancipated and left to themselves, are
worthless and helpless, and are sure, in the end, to become a burden on the community. But the commission
has not found, in a single locality occupied by numbers
of free negroes, proof that there is truth in such an
opinion; on the contrary, the actual facts are against
it. In many free States, colored immigrants are required by law to give bond that they will not become
a county charge. There is no class of day-laborers
from whom, with equal justice, the same demand might
not be made.

---

* See pages 119–122, *ante.*

There came to the knowledge of our commission, in New Orleans, a fact which, more strikingly perhaps than any other we have met with, bears testimony to the ability of the colored population, when emancipated, to take care of themselves.*

The commission ascertained that the free colored people of Louisiana, in the year 1860, paid taxes on an assessment of thirteen millions. But, by the census of 1860, the free colored population of that State is put at eighteen thousand six hundred and forty-seven. This would give an average, for each person, of about seven hundred dollars of property.

It is probable, however, that the actual average is considerably less than this. Those best informed on the subject expressed to a member of the commission who visited New Orleans the opinion that the census-return was below the truth, and that in 1860 there were probably in Louisiana twenty-five thousand free colored persons. Assuming this to be the actual number, then the average wealth of each is *five hundred and twenty dollars.*

But the average amount of property to each person throughout the loyal Free States is estimated at four hundred and eighty-four dollars only.† It follows that the free colored people of Louisiana are, on the average, richer, by seven and a half per cent., than the people of the Northern States. And this occurs, it should be remembered, under many civil disabilities, which are a great pecuniary injury, seriously restricting the means of accumulating property.

---

* Supplemental Report (B) on the Lower Mississippi, by James McKaye.

† See, for the above estimates of average wealth and of population, "National Almanac for 1863," pp. 117, 309. The average wealth in Great Britain and Ireland is *seven hundred and seven dollars* for each person.—*Same Almanac,* p. 146.

It is not as individuals only, but, so far as they have had opportunity to show it, in a collective capacity, that these people appear to manage well. We have the following testimony from a well-known and respected citizen of Louisville :—

Question.—" Throughout the State do the colored people manage their own church affairs?"

Answer.—" Entirely. Nobody has any thing to do with them but themselves. Here is a curious fact to show what their capacity is. A great many of the churches now owned by them had been failures in the hands of white people. The negroes bought and paid for them, and have improved them very much since the purchase. Mr. Adams's church is a much finer one now than when we sold it to them. Mr. Smethern's church was built by white people, who we ·e not able to pay for it, and was then bought by t.ıc negroes. Nobody would suppose it now to be the same house, its appearance is so much changed for the better. And that is very common. They have much taste about such things."*

Upon the whole, no fear is more groundless than that the result of Emancipation will be to throw the negroes as a burden on the community.

---

* The deponent is Dr. T. S. Bell.—(Testimony taken by the Commission in Kentucky, p. 17.)

CHAPTER IV.

THE EMANCIPATED NEGRO WILL MAKE THE SOUTH HIS HOME.

THERE is another popular idea, in regard to the effect of Emancipation, which has been used for political effect. This idea is based on an imaginary state of things which happens to be the very reverse of the truth. It is alleged that so soon as the negroes are freed they will swarm to the North in search of work, and thus become the competitors of the laboring whites. Beyond all doubt they have a right to do this; and, if they did, no just man would complain of it. But, in point of fact, no such thing will happen, *unless Emancipation be denied.*

Of this the commission collected abundant proof: for example, in visiting the freedmen of South Carolina. General Saxton, who had there eighteen thousand emancipated slaves under his care, offered them papers to go North, but not one availed himself of the offer. They are equally averse to the idea of emigrating to Africa.* Colonization, except by force (and that would be an outrage), is utterly impracticable. These feelings are universal among them. The local attachments of the negro are eminently strong, and the Southern climate suits him far better than ours.

---

* The following testimony was taken by the commission in Louisville:—
Colonel Hodges, who had lived all his life among slaves, deposed, "The State of Kentucky has appropriated five thousand dollars a year for several years to aid the Colonization Society in sending off the free blacks, but they have never been able to get *more than two* to apply."—*Testimony taken in Kentucky,* p. 104.

If we could suppose slavery re-established in the insurrectionary States, the North would indeed be flooded with fugitives fleeing from bondage, and the fears of competition in labor sought to be excited in the minds of Northern working-men might then have some plausible foundation. But, if Emancipation be carried out, the stream of negro emigration will be from the North to the South, not from the South to the Northern States. The only attraction which the North, with its winters of snow and ice, offers to the negro, is that it is free soil. Let the South once offer the same attraction, and the temptation of its genial climate, coupled with the fact that there the blacks almost equal the whites in number, will be irresistible. A few years will probably see more than half the free negro population now residing among us crossing Mason and Dixon's line, to join the emancipated freedmen of the South. A primary law governing the voluntary movements of peoples is that of thermal lines.

The commission found overwhelming evidence, as to the truth of the above opinion, in Canada West. Among the refugees there, there is not a single feeling so strong or so nearly universal as their longing to return to the Southern land of their birth, at the earliest moment when they shall be assured that it is purged from slavery. One of the commission thus states the result of his observations:—

"If slavery is utterly abolished in the United States, no more colored people will emigrate to Canada, and most of those now there will soon leave it. There can be no doubt about this. Among the hundreds who spoke about it, only one dissented from the strong expression of desire to 'go home.' In their belief, too, they agreed with the Rev. Mr. Kinnard, one of their clergy, who said to us, 'If freedom is established in the United States, there will be one great black streak reaching from here to the uttermost parts of the South.'"*

Even those who, by years of toil, have obtained comfortable, well-stocked farms worth ten or twenty thousand dollars, avowed their determination to abandon all—to sell out and depart—as soon as they could do so without imperilling their personal freedom.

Emancipation will directly tend to denude the North of its negro population. One circumstance that will materially hasten this result is that the personal prejudice against negroes, as a race, is stronger in the Northern than in the Southern States, and at least as strong in Canada as in any portion of the Union. Of this our commission had sufficient proof.

Mr. George Brown, a member of the Canadian Parliament, deposed, before the commission, "I think the prejudice against the colored people is stronger here than in the States."†

Mr. Sinclair, of Chatham (Canada West), said, "Many of the colored people, even in this town, say that, if they could have the same privileges in the States that they have here, they would not remain here a moment. * * * In this county there is one township (that of Orford) where no colored man is allowed to settle."‡

The colored people of Canada themselves testified to the same effect. Mrs. Brown, of St. Catherine's, deposed, "I find more prejudice here than I did in York State. When I was at home, I could go anywhere; but here,— my goodness! you get an insult on every side."§

Mrs. Susan Boggs (colored), also of St. Catherine's, said, "If it was not for the queen's law, we would be

---

* Supplemental Report (A) on Refugees in Canada West, p. 28.
† Ibid. p. 43.　　　　‡ Ibid. p. 43.　　　　§ Ibid. p. 44.

mobbed here, and could not stay in this house. The prejudice is a great deal worse here than it is in the States."*

A colored woman living in a cabin near Colchester said "she was from Virginia, and the prejudice was a 'heap' stronger in Canada than at home." "The people," she added, "seemed to think the blacks weren't folks, anyway." She was anxious to go back.†

The home of the American negro is in the Southern States. Let it be made a free home, and he will seek —he will desire—no other.

. Whether, as a freedman in a Southern home, the negro will live down the cruel prejudice which has followed him, increasing in virulence, to a British province, some, with De Tocqueville, will continue to doubt. But powerful agencies are at work in his favor,—some of terrible character. Such were the New York riots. Such, more recently, were the atrocities committed at Fort Pillow.

We have found ourselves called upon to interpose in favor of the outraged and the unprotected. But such interposition tends to create, even in minds of ordinary sensibility, good will and sympathy towards the sufferers whom one interposes to protect.

It will have a tendency to increase harmony between the two races, if the colored people, whether in the North or the South, refrain from settling in colonies or suburbs by themselves; for such separation tends to keep up alienation of feeling and to nourish the prejudices of race. They will do well, therefore, to mingle their dwellings or farms with those of the whites; for the effect of this will be to take off the edge of national prejudice and weaken the feeling which regards them as a separate and alien race.

CHAPTER V.

AMALGAMATION.

SOME may be of opinion that the effect of such commingling will be to introduce amalgamation between the races; others, that such amalgamation is the natural and proper solution of the problem. I believe neither the one nor the other.

In the first place, such evidence in this matter as our commission has obtained goes to show that, at least in a Northern climate, the mixed race is inferior, in physical power and in health, to the pure race, black or white. A member of our commission carefully investigated the condition of the refugees of mixed blood in Canada, and took evidence as to their health, physical stamina, and power of increase. He found them mostly of lymphatic temperament, with marks of scrofulous or strumous disposition, as shown in the pulpy appearance of portions of the face and neck, in the spongy gums and glistering teeth. There is a general prevalence of phthisical diseases.*

Dr. Mack, of St. Catherine's, testified, "The mixed race are the most unhealthy, and the pure blacks the least so. The disease they suffer most from is pulmonary. Where there is not real tubercular affection of the lungs, there are bronchitis and pulmonary affections. I have the idea that they die out when mixed, and that this climate will completely efface them. I think the pure blacks will live."†

---

* Supplemental Report (A), p. 21.　　　　　† Ibid. p. 23.

General Tullock, of the British Army, one of the authors of four volumes of military statistics, writes to one of the members of our commission, "The mulatto race are seldom employed in our army, chiefly owing to the want of that physical stamina which renders the pure negro better fitted for the duties of a soldier or a laborer."*

Dr. Fisher, of Malden, Canada, thinks that the mulattoes of Canada cannot maintain their numbers without assistance from emigration.†

This is in accordance with the census-returns of the free colored population in some of the Northern States, where most of them are of mixed blood. A member of the commission prepared a table of the births, marriages, and deaths among the colored population of Boston for eight years,—namely, from 1855 to 1862, both inclusive. It shows three hundred and four births, three hundred and sixteen marriages, and five hundred deaths. In every one of these years the deaths exceeded the births, and in 1855, 1858, and 1860, the births were less than the marriages. This is the more remarkable when we take into account what the register of the city, in furnishing the above table, states,—namely, that the number of marriages among the colored people was fifty per cent. more, in proportion to population, than among the whites,—being among the former 1 in 58, and among the latter only 1 in 87.54.‡

The United States census for 1860 shows, in several of the other States, similar results. In Providence, the deaths among the free colored are over four per cent. a year. In Philadelphia, during the six months preceding the census, there were among these people one hundred and forty-eight births to three hundred and

---

* Supplemental Report (A), p. 26.   † Ibid. p. 26.   ‡ Ibid. pp. 23, 24.

six deaths,—the deaths being more than double the births.*

The same census shows that the total free colored population of the Union has increased about one per cent. a year during the last decade; and this includes slaves liberated, and slaves escaped from their masters, during that period. The actual rate of natural increase is certainly less than half that of the slaves, which from 1850 to 1860 was 23.38 per cent.,—say two and a third per cent. annually.

It is sometimes inferred from this that the slaves live in greater comfort than the free colored people, and that the latter cannot take as good care of themselves as masters take of their slaves. But the facts which have come to our knowledge touching the actual condition of these two classes, the slave and the free colored, are wholly at variance with any such conclusion. We believe the chief reason of the small rate of increase to be, that the proportion of mulattoism among the free colored is much greater than among slaves, and that the mulattoes, certainly in northern latitudes, are less healthy and prolific than the pure blacks.

In support of the opinion that the same may be predicated of these two classes in Southern States, it may be alleged that a cold climate is, in all probability, as little suited to the pure black, originally from the torrid zones of Africa, as to the mulatto, with a cross of Anglo-Saxon blood; and that if, even in such a climate, the mortality among the mixed race is greater than among pure blacks, the climate is not likely to be the sole cause.

It is certain, however, that both as regards blacks and mulattoes, their mortality as compared with whites

---

* Preliminary Report of the Eighth Census, 1860, p. 6.

essentially depends upon climate. As this is an important matter, our commission spent considerable time and labor in collecting reliable statistics which throw light upon it.* The table on the opposite page—the most exhaustive summary, probably, that has yet been made public, in connection with this subject—was carefully made up from the materials obtained.

The total sum of white lives upon which the above calculations are based, is, as will be observed, upwards of thirty-seven millions,—of colored lives, upwards of three millions; while the deaths among whites are over one million, and among the colored over a hundred thousand. The general inference from records on so large a scale may be taken as substantially correct, even if we admit the probability of partial inaccuracies in some of the returns.

Thus we reach several interesting facts. The rate of annual deaths among the whites is less than two and three-quarters per cent., or about one to every thirty-seven of the living; among the colored about three and a half per cent., or one in every twenty-eight [or, exactly, 1 in 37.57 whites against 1 in 28.54 colored].

I remark, further, that the mortality diminishes as we approach our own time,—in Boston especially. In that city, between 1725 and 1774, the average annual mortality was, among whites, 1 in 29.10, and, among colored, 1 in 14.9; whereas from 1855 to 1862 it was but 1 in 43 among whites, and 1 in 31 among colored. This accords with the well-known fact that the average

---

* In this they have been greatly aided by Dr. Edward Jarvis, of Boston. That gentleman not only kindly opened to the commission the treasures of his valuable statistical library, but has personally superintended some of the researches touching this matter.

Table of Comparative Mortality among White and Colored Persons in Eleven Cities of the United States.

Place.	Period.	No. of years.	Sum of Annual Population. White.	Colored.	Number of Deaths. White.	Colored.	Pop. to one Death. White.	Colored.
Boston......	1725 to 1774,	57	639,000	59,500	23,750	4,000	29.10	14.90
"	1855–59, 1861–62. {		1,188,452	15,620	27,522	500	43.18	31.24
New Bedford.....	1861–62–63	3	65,259	4,746	1,500	179	42.09	26.51
Providence......	1810 to 1863	24	958,028	35,349	20,744	1,306	46.25	27.06
New York......	1821, 1824–29, 1831–36, 1838–62...	38	15,427,166	531,514	479,879	20,428	32.14	25.39
Buffalo......	1854–58, 1862–63......	7	530,582	5,466	14,013	120	37.86	45.55*
Philadelphia	1821 to 1862......	42	12,466,457	750,996	269,824	26,397	46.22	28.45
Baltimore......	1818, 1821–25, 1827–29, 1833–34, 1836–63......	38	4,294,476	859,025	107,623	26,551	39.90	32.34
Washington......	1849–60......	12	455,754	126,305	8,869	2,723	51.38	46.36†
Charleston......	1828–57......	30	457,756	523,536	13,915	10,868	32.83	31.03
New Orleans......	1849–50, 1856, and ⅔ of 1855, 1860.	43	547,523	121,343	32,143	6,277	17.03	19.51
Memphis......	1851–53......	3	24,126	8,043	1,406	428	17.17	18.79
Eleven cities, total	......		37,104,879	3,031,473	1,001,268	106,217	37.57 Per ct. 2.699	28.54 Per ct. 3.503

* This being the sole exception, among Northern cities, to what seems the general rule, to wit: that the mortality among blacks is much greater than among whites, we may reasonably suppose some inaccuracy in returns.

† The great apparent salubrity among both classes in Washington is not, probably, to be ascribed either to the climate or the mode of life, but to the fact that a large proportion of the population are mere sojourners there, for a few years during the working period of life, when the rate of mortality is lowest.

length of life in the United States is greater in this century than it was in the last.

Again, the table shows that the mortality among blacks in the Northern cities is considerably greater than among whites; while in the Southern cities it averages about the same.

As the returns from which this table is compiled do not distinguish between blacks and mulattoes, it gives us no information as to the relative mortality among these two classes. On that point it behooves us to abstain from confident generalizing in the absence of more exact and more extended statistical data.

This, however, we may say :—It would appear that there are certain races of men the cross between which produces a race quite equal to either of the progenitors. This is said to be true of the Turk and the African. It may be that the Anglo-Saxon and the African, extreme varieties, are less suited to each other, and that the mixed race degenerates. Indeed, so far as a limited range of facts go, there seems a probability in favor of the opinion expressed by a member of the commission, that "the mulatto, considered in his animal nature, lacks the innervation and spring of the pure blacks and whites," and that "the organic inferiority is shown in less power of resisting destructive agencies, in less fecundity and less longevity."*

If this be so, then amalgamation of these two races is in itself a physical evil injurious to both,—a practice which ought to be discouraged by public opinion, and avoided by all who consider it a duty, as parents, to transmit to their offspring the best conditions for sound health and physical well-being. Like other evils

---

* Supplemental Report (A), p. 27.

of the kind, however, this is beyond the legitimate reach of legislation.

I believe that the effect of general emancipation will be to discourage amalgamation. It is rare in Canada; and public opinion there, among blacks as well as whites, is against it.

Bishop Green, of the Methodist Church, Canada, deposed, "You do not see any of our respectable people here marrying any persons but their own associates." John Kinney, an intelligent colored man, said, "The majority of the colored people don't like the intermarriage of colored and white people." Colonel Stevenson said, "The colored people don't like to have one of their color marry a white woman." Such marriages do occur in Canada, but they are rare.*

De Tocqueville had already remarked that emancipation, which might be supposed to favor amalgamation, does, in point of fact, repress it.†

Amalgamation, in its worst form, is the offspring of slavery. The facts seem to indicate that, with the abolition of slavery, it will materially diminish, though it may be doubted whether it will ever wholly disappear.

CHAPTER VI.

RECIPROCAL SOCIAL INFLUENCE OF THE RACES ON EACH OTHER.

ASIDE from this apparently injurious mingling of blood, the social influence of the two races on each other, so soon as their reciprocal relations are based

---

* Supplemental Report (A), pp. 30, 31.
† Democracy in America, vol. i. p. 462.

on justice, will, beyond question, be mutually bene-
ficial. There are elements in the character of each
calculated to exert a happy influence on the other.

The Anglo-Saxon race, with great force of character,
much mental activity, an unflagging spirit of enterprise, has a certain hardness, a stubborn will, only
moderate geniality, a lack of habitual cheerfulness.
Its intellectual powers are stronger than its social instincts. The head predominates over the heart. There
is little that is emotional in its religion. It is not devoid of instinctive devotion; but neither is such devotion a ruling element. It is a race more calculated to
call forth respect than love; better fitted to do than
to enjoy.

The African race is in many respects the reverse
of this. Genial, lively, docile, emotional, the affections rule; the social instincts maintain the ascend-
ant. Except under cruel repression, its cheerfulness
and love of mirth overflow with the exuberance of
childhood. It is devotional by feeling. It is a knowing rather than a thinking race. Its perceptive facul-
ties are stronger than its reflective powers. It is well
fitted to occupy useful stations in life,—but such as require quick observation rather than comprehensive
views or strong sense. It is little given to stirring enterprise, but rather to quiet accumulation. It is not a
race that will ever take a lead in the material improvement of the world; but it will make for itself, whenever it has fair play, respectable positions, comfortable
homes.*

---

* "The surest sign of their thrift is the appearance of their dwelling-
houses, farms, stock, tools, and the like. In these, moreover, we find en-
couraging signs for the negro, because they show that he feels so strongly
the family instinct and the desire to possess land and a dwelling-place."—
Supplemental Report (A), p. 62.

As regards the virtues of humility, loving-kindness, resignation under adversity, reliance on Divine Providence, this race exhibits these, as a general rule, in a more marked manner than does the Anglo-Saxon. Nor do we find among them a spirit of revenge or bloodthirstiness or rancorous ill will towards their oppressors.* The exceptions to this rule, notwithstanding the great temptations to which the race have been exposed, are very rare. No race of men appears better to have obeyed the injunction not to return evil for evil, or to have acted more strictly in the spirit of the text, "Vengeance is mine; I will repay, saith the Lord."

With time, as civilization advances, these Christian graces of meekness and long-suffering will be rated higher than the world rates them now. With time, if we but treat these people in a Christian spirit, we shall have our reward. The softening influence of their genial spirit, diffused throughout the community, will make itself felt as an element of improvement in the national character.

And, on the other hand, they will learn much and gain much from us. They will gain in force of character, in mental cultivation, in self-reliance, in enter-

* "Canada is full of men and women who in the first half of their lives were witnesses and sufferers of such indignities and wrongs as would burn into most white men's souls and make them pass the last half in plotting vengeance. Not so these people. They cherish no spirit of vengeance, and seem to have no grudge against their oppressors. The memory and recital of their wrongs do not arouse such bitter feelings and call out such maledictions as would certainly be heard from white men of similar experience. A single instance only is recollected in which a feeling of unsatisfied vengeance was manifested; but many are recalled where the old master and mistress were spoken of with kindness, and regret expressed that they would not be seen again."—*Supplemental Report* (A), pp. 97, 98.

prise, in breadth of views, and in habits of generaliza-
tion. Our influence over them, if we treat them well,
will be powerful for good.*

CHAPTER VII.

IMPORTANCE, NATIONALLY, THAT THE NEGRO BE TREATED WITH JUSTICE.

THE last sentence contains an important proviso.
If we treat them well! Every thing depends upon
that. There depends upon it not alone the future of
four millions and a half of people, native-born, and
who will remain, for good or for evil, in the land of
their birth, but also, looking to the immediate present,
there depends, to a certain extent, the likelihood of
thoroughly and speedily putting down the present
rebellion.

Every aggression, every act of injustice committed
by a Northern man against unoffending fugitives from
despotism, every insult offered by the base prejudice
of our race to a colored man because of his African descent, is not only a breach of humanity, an offence
against civilization, but it is also an act which gives
aid and comfort to the enemy. The report of it goes
abroad,—penetrates into the enemy's country. So far
as its influence there extends, the effect is to deter the
slave from leaving his master,—therefore to secure to

---

* Mr. McCullum, principal of the High School, Hamilton, Canada, said,
" Colored people brought up among whites look better than others.
Their rougher, harsher features disappear. I think that colored children
brought up among white people look better than their parents."—*Supplemental Report (A),* p. 79.

that master a bread-producer, and, by the same act, to deprive the Union of a colored soldier, and force the Government to withdraw a laborer, in his stead, from a Northern farm.

The practical effect, therefore, of abuse and injury to colored people, in these days, is not alone to disgrace the authors of such acts, but to compel conscription, and to strip the North—already scant of working-hands—of the laborers and the artisans that remain to her. Thousands of fields owned by white men may remain untilled, thousands of hearths owned by white men may be made desolate,—all as the direct result of the ill treatment of the colored race.

Such a spirit is not treasonable, in the usual sense of that term; yet its results are the same as those of treason itself. It becomes, therefore, in a military point of view, of the highest importance that all wanton acts of aggression by soldiers or civilians, whether against refugees or against free negroes heretofore settled in the North, should be promptly and resolutely repressed, and the penalties of the law in every such case rigorously enforced. A prudent regard for our own safety and welfare, if no higher motive prompt, demands the taking of such precaution.

We have imposed upon ourselves an additional obligation to see justice and humanity exercised towards these people, in accepting their services as soldiers. It would be a degree of baseness of which I hope our country is incapable, to treat with contumely the defenders of the Union,—the men who shall have confronted death on the battle-field, side by side with the bravest of our own race, in a struggle in which the stake is the existence, in peace and in their integrity, of these United States.

We are unjust to our enemies if we deny that this struggle has been a hard-fought one, contested bravely and with varying success. A people with an element of semi-barbarism in their society, giving birth to habits of violence and of lawless daring, are in some respects better prepared for war than one which stands on a higher plane of Christian civilization.

There is an additional reason why a considerable portion of the Union armies should be made up of persons of African descent. The eradication of negro slavery has become a necessity of our national existence. But the history of the world furnishes no example of an enslaved race which won its freedom without exertion of its own. That the indiscriminate massacres of a servile insurrection have been spared us, as addition to the horrors of a civil war, is due, it would seem, rather to that absence of revenge and bloodthirstiness which characterizes this race, than to the lack either of courage or of any other quality that makes the hardy combatant; for these the negro appears, so far as we have tried him in civilized warfare, to possess. And in such warfare it is fitting that the African race seek its own social salvation. The negro must fight for emancipation if he is to be emancipated.

If, then, emancipation be the price of national unity and of peace, and if a people, to be emancipated, must draw the sword in their own cause, then is the future welfare of the white race in our country indissolubly connected with an act of justice, on our part, towards people of another race; then is it the sole condition under which we may expect—and, if history speak truth, the sole condition under which we shall attain—domestic tranquillity, that we shall give the negro an opportunity of working out, on those battle-fields that are to decide our own national destiny, *his* destiny, whether as slave or as freedman, at the same time.

But, to give full scope to the energies of this race in war, we must not treat them as step-children. It is so manifestly just, to say nothing of the evident expediency for the benefit of the service, that no discrimination should be made, either as to pay or in any other respect, between the white and the colored soldier, that I deem it hardly necessary to express the conviction that of all petty schemes of false economy such discrimination against the colored soldier is the worst. Performing the same duties, subjected to the same fatigues, marshalled on the same battle-fields, side by side with the white soldier, and exposing, like him, his life for his country, one would think that the innate sense of right would preclude the necessity of a single argument on the subject. What probability of future harmony between the races, if we begin our connection with the new-made freedmen by such an act of flagrant injustice?

Let us beware the temptation to treat the colored people with less than even justice because they have been, and still are, lowly and feeble. Let us bear in mind that with governments, as with individuals, the crucial test of civilization and sense of justice is their treatment of the weak and the dependent.

God is offering to us an opportunity of atoning, in some measure, to the African for our former complicity in his wrongs. For our own sakes as well as for his, let it not be lost. As we would that He should be to us and to our children, so let us be to those whose dearest interests are by His providence committed, for the time, to our charge.

CHAPTER VIII.

THE FREEDMAN NEEDS MERE TEMPORARY AID OR SUPERVISION.

As regards the question what amount of aid and interference is necessary or desirable to enable the freedmen to tide over the stormy transition from slavery to freedom, it is certain that there is as much danger in doing too much as in doing too little. The risk is serious that, under the guise of guardianship, slavery, in a modified form, may be practically restored. Those who have ceased only perforce to be slaveholders will be sure to unite their efforts to effect just such a purpose. It should be the earnest object of all friends of liberty to anticipate and prevent it. Benevolence itself, misdirected, may play into the hands of freedom's enemies; and those whose earnest endeavor is the good of the freedman may unconsciously contribute to his virtual re-enslavement.

The refugees from slavery, when they first cross our lines, need temporary aid, but not more than indigent Southern whites fleeing from secessionism,—both being sufferers from the disturbance of labor and the destruction of its products incident to war. The families of colored men, hired as military laborers or enlisted as soldiers, need protection and assistance, but not more than the families of white men similarly situated. Forcibly deprived of education in a state of slavery, the freedmen have a claim upon us to lend a helping hand until they can organize schools for their children. But they will soon take the labor and expense out of our hands; for these people pay no charge more willingly than that which assures them that their children shall reap those advantages of instruction which were denied to themselves.

If we organize a Freedman's Bureau, it should be borne in mind that we need its agency as a temporary alleviation, not because these people are negroes, only because they are men who have been, for generations, deprived of their rights.

Extensive experience in the West Indies has proved that Emancipation, when it takes place, should be unconditional and absolute. The experiment of a few years' apprenticeship, plausible in theory, proved in practice a failure so injurious in its effects that the provincial legislatures, though they had been opposed to the abolition of slavery, voted, after trial, for the abolition of a 'prenticeship.

The freedman should be treated at once as any other free man. He should be subjected to no compulsory contracts as to labor. There should not be, directly or indirectly, any statutory rates of wages. There should be no interference between the hirers and the hired. Nor should any restrictions be imposed in regard to the local movements of these people, except such regulations incident to war, relative to vagrancy or otherwise, as apply equally to whites. The natural laws of supply and demand should be left, in all cases, to regulate rates of compensation and places of residence.

When freedmen shall have voluntarily entered into any agreement to work, they may, at first, usefully be aided in reducing that agreement to writing, and, for a time, we may properly see to it that such freedmen do not suffer from ill treatment or failure of contract on the part of their employers, and that they themselves perform their duty in the premises.

But all aid given to these people should be regarded

as a temporary necessity; all supervision over them should be provisional only, and advisory in its character. The sooner they can learn to stand alone and to make their own unaided way, the better both for our race and for theirs.

CHAPTER IX.

THE SUM OF OUR DUTY TOWARDS THE NEGRO RACE.

THE essential is, that we secure to them the means of making their own way,—that we give them, to use the familiar phrase, "a fair chance." If, like whites, they are to be self-supporting, then, like whites, they ought to have those rights, civil and political, without which they are but laboring as a man labors with hands bound.

There will, for some time to come, be a tendency, on the part of many among those who have heretofore held them in bondage, still to treat them in an unjust and tyrannical manner. The effectual remedy for this is not special enactments, or a special permanent organization, for the protection of colored people, but the safeguard of general laws, applicable to all, against fraud and oppression.

The sum of our recommendations is this. Offer the freedmen temporary aid and counsel, until they become a little accustomed to their new sphere of life; secure to them, by law, their just rights of person and property; relieve them, by a fair and equal administration of justice, from the depressing influence of disgraceful prejudice; above all, guard them against the virtual restoration of slavery, in any form, under any pretext; and then let them take care of themselves.

If we do this, the future of the African race in this country will be conducive to its prosperity and associated with its well-being. There will be nothing connected with it to excite regret or inspire apprehension.

20

APPENDIX.

NOTE A. (Page 61.)

SINCE the calculations in the text relative to the mortality chargeable to the African slave-trade and to the number of slaves imported were made, some confirmatory documents have come under my observation.

I had assumed, as the average deportation of slaves, one hundred and twenty thousand a year from 1788 to 1840; and sixty-five thousand a year only from 1840 to 1848 (pp. 36 and 37). Mr. Buxton, in his African Slave-Trade, after supplying elaborate details, thus sums up the total for 1839, the year in which he wrote:—

"I limit myself to the facts which I have established,—namely:—

That there are at the present time annually imported into Brazil	78,333
That the annual importations into Cuba amount to	60,000
That there have been captured	8,294
And I assume that the casualties amount to	3,373
Making together	150,000*"

This estimate is for those *actually landed*. As Mr. Buxton estimates (p. 169) the number lost on the passage at twenty-five per cent. on those landed (or thirty-seven thousand five hundred out of one hundred and fifty thousand), this gives

---

* The African Slave-Trade, by **Thomas Fowell Buxton**, London, 1839, p. 26.

his estimate of the deportation from Africa in the year 1839 at one hundred and eighty-seven thousand five hundred.

And this was at the time when two nations only, Brazil and Spain, remained as customers of the slaver. The estimate is at least double mine.

Mr. Buxton's estimate agrees with mine in the calculation that for every negro shipped, another "must have been sacrificed in the seizure, march, and detention."—p. 169.

He calculates, further, that of those actually landed, "twenty per cent. die in the seasoning."—p. 169.

He quotes the celebrated William Pitt, as saying, during the debate on the slave-trade in 1791, "The evidence before the House as to the mortality was perfectly clear; for it would be found in that dreadful catalogue of deaths in consequence of the seasoning and the Middle Passage, which the House had been condemned to look into, that *one-half die*."—pp. 160, 161.

Various travellers in Africa furnish items going to show the loss of life in Africa, as compared to the slaves obtained.

Denham, the noted traveller, says, "In one instance twenty thousand were killed for sixteen thousand carried away into slavery." In another case, "*probably more than double*" *the number of those captured were killed by the captors.**

Dr. Holroyd, an African traveller who returned from Nubia and Cordofan in 1838, wrote, under date January 14, to Mr. Buxton:—"There is not only a terrible waste of life in the attempts to capture the negroes, but after they are seized there is so much of ill usage and brutality that I have been assured no less than thirty per cent. perish in the first ten days after their seizure."—*Buxton's African Slave-Trade*, p. 84.

The Rev. John Newton, Rector of St. Mary's, Woolworth, who in early life was engaged in the slave-trade, and afterwards published a work on the subject, after expressing the opinion that the "far greater part of the wars in Africa would cease if Europeans would cease to tempt them by offering goods for slaves," adds, "*I believe the captives reserved for sale are fewer than the slain*."—*Newton on the Slave-Trade*, London, 1788, p. 30.

---

* Denham & Clapperton's Travels in Africa, London, 1826, pp. 116, 214.

Evidence of a similar character might be indefinitely multiplied. But I close with an incident related, from personal observation, by one of our own countrymen. Mr. Ashman, agent of the American Colonial Society, writing from Liberia in 1823, says:—

"The following incident I relate not for its singularity, for similar events take place, perhaps, every month in the year, but it has fallen under my own observation, and I can vouch for its authenticity. King Boatswain, our most powerful supporter and steady friend among the natives, received a quantity of goods on trust from a French slaver, for which he stipulated to pay young slaves. He makes it a point of honor to be punctual to his engagements. The time was at hand when he expected the return of the slaver, and he had not the slaves. Looking around on the peaceful tribes about him for his victims, he singled out the Queaks, a small agricultural and trading people, of most inoffensive character. His warriors were skilfully distributed to the different hamlets, and, making a simultaneous assault on the sleeping occupants in the dead of the night, accomplished, without difficulty or resistance, in one hour, the annihilation of the whole tribe! Every adult man and woman was murdered,—every hut fired! Very young children generally shared the fate of their parents. The boys and girls alone were reserved to pay the Frenchman." —Ashman's *Life*, New York, 1835, p. 160.

20*

NOTE B. (Page 192.)

An act of general emancipation, with appropriate preamble, might be couched somewhat in the terms following:—

A Bill to Emancipate Persons of African Descent held to Service or Labor in certain of the United States.

Whereas there is now flagrant, in certain of the United States, an insurrection of proportions so gigantic that there has been required, to hold it in check, an increase of the army and navy of the United States to an extent seldom paralleled in the history of the world;

And whereas, because of the said insurrection, the execution of the laws for collecting taxes, and of various other laws of the United States, heretofore enacted by the Congress in the just exercise of their constitutional powers, has been, for more than two years past, and still is, obstructed and defeated throughout the insurrectionary States;

And whereas it is the right and duty of the Congress to make all laws which shall be necessary and proper for carrying into execution the said constitutional powers;

And whereas the said insurrectionary portions of the Union consist exclusively of States wherein persons of African descent are held in large numbers to involuntary service or labor, the white inhabitants thereof basing their insurrectionary acts upon the assumption that the security and perpetuation of such involuntary servitude require the disruption of the national unity, and the establishment, on a portion of the domain of the United States, of a separate and independent government;

And whereas a large portion of the said persons of African descent, so held in servitude, contribute greatly, so long as such involuntary services are thus exacted from them, to the aid and comfort of the said insurgents, laboring for their behoof on their fortifications and for the supply of their commissariat, and otherwise giving strength and support to various insurrectionary acts;

And whereas, in an emergency so urgent as that which is now patent to the world, it is the duty of the Congress to place at the disposal of the Executive branch of the Government, for the common defence, the utmost power, civil and military, of the country, and to employ every means not forbidden by the usages of civilized warfare, and not in violation of the Constitution, that is placed within their reach, in order to repress and to bring to a speedy termination the present protracted and desolating insurrection;

And whereas it appears, from the above recitals, that the existence, within any portion of the United States, of a labor-system which recognizes the claims of one race of men to the involuntary services of another race (always a moral wrong) has now shown itself to be destructive of the supremacy of the laws, and a constant menace to the Government, and that the continuance of such labor-system imminently jeopardizes the integrity of the Union, and has become incompatible with the domestic tranquillity of the country;

And whereas it has thus become evident that claims to the involuntary service or labor of persons of African descent ought not to be possessed by any inhabitant of the United States, but should, in the just exercise of the power which inheres in every independent government to protect itself from destruction by seizing and destroying any private property of its citizens or subjects which imperils its own existence, be taken, for public use, from their present possessors, and abrogated and annulled,—just compensation being made to so many of the said possessors of such claims, not being nor having been public enemies, as may demand it, and as may by their loyalty be entitled thereto, for the claims so abrogated and annulled;

And whereas the President of the United States, by Proclamation of January 1, 1863, did declare that all persons held as slaves within the States of Arkansas, Texas, Louisiana, Mississippi, Alabama, Florida, Georgia, South Carolina, North Carolina, and Virginia (certain parishes in Louisiana and certain counties in Virginia excepted) were on that day, and thenceforth forever should be, free; therefore

Be it enacted by the Senate and House of Representatives in Congress assembled, That the action of the President, as Commander-in-Chief of the Army and Navy of the United States, in issuing his Proclamation of January 1, 1863, as a fit and necessary war measure for the suppression of the existing insurrection, is hereby approved and endorsed, and the emancipation of the slaves thereby effected is recognized and declared to be an act just, legal, and irrevocable.

SEC. 2. *And be it further enacted,* That from and after the fourth of July next, all claims to the service or labor of persons of African descent, who shall then be held to involuntary labor in any of the States of the Union under the laws thereof, be and the same are hereby taken by the Government of the United States. And the said claims are hereby abrogated and annulled. And all persons of African descent within the United States who shall, on the said fourth day of July next, be held to involuntary service or labor except for crime of which the party shall have been legally convicted, shall be released and emancipated from such claims in as full and complete a manner as if the same had never existed; the said release and emancipation to take effect from and after the said fourth day of July, thenceforth and for evermore.

SEC. 3. *And be it further enacted,* That the faith of the United States be and the same is hereby pledged for the payment of just compensation to all persons who shall, on the said fourth day of July, hold such claims to service or labor; provided, that such persons shall make application for such compensation in form and manner hereinafter to be prescribed; and provided, further, that such persons are not nor have not been, in law, public enemies of the United States; and provided, further, that said persons shall have been, throughout the present insurrection, true and loyal to the Government of the United States, and shall not, directly or indirectly, have incited to insurrectionary acts, or given aid or comfort to any persons engaged in the insurrection aforesaid.

An act couched in the terms here proposed could not be

declared unconstitutional by the Supreme Court without a reckless reversal of principles as well established, and of as high authority, as any which form the basis of constitutional law, nor without an encroachment on legislative ground so flagrant that it might well subject those members of the court who should give it their official sanction to impeachment, on the charge of usurpation.

INDEX.

246　　　　　　　　　　INDEX.

THE END.

www.ingramcontent.com/pod-product-compliance
Lightning Source LLC
Chambersburg PA
CBHW030402270326
41926CB00009B/1227